50 THINGS TO BAKE

✦ Before You Die ✦

THE WORLD'S BEST CAKES, PIES, BROWNIES, COOKIES, AND MORE FROM YOUR FAVORITE BAKERS, INCLUDING CHRISTINA TOSI, JOANNE CHANG, AND DOMINIQUE ANSEL

BY ALLYSON REEDY

Select Photography by Greg McBoat

ULYSSES PRESS

Published by:
Ulysses Press
PO Box 3440
Berkeley, CA 94703
www.ulyssespress.com

ISBN: 978-1-64604-331-6
Library of Congress Control Number: 2021946400

Printed in the United States by Versa Press
10 9 8 7 6 5 4 3 2 1

Acquisitions: Casie Vogel
Managing editor: Claire Chun
Project editor: Kierra Sondereker
Proofreader: Phyllis Elving
Front cover and interior design: Raquel Castro
Layout: Jake Flaherty
Interior photography: Greg McBoat except page 31 © Cambrea Gordon; page 32 © Ashley Maxwell; page 35 © Erica Schroeder; page 42 © Milk Bar; page 44 © Trina Harris; page 55 © Sugar Geek Show; page 70 © Brett Field; page 77 © Alexandra Shytsman; page 78 © Upper Crust; page 82 © Anthony Delao; page 89 © Vanessa Mir Heirloomsnaps; page 90 © Wendy Kelley; page 103 © Evan Sung; page 112 © Katina Talley; page 116 © Kimberlee Ho; page 119 © Elizabeth Beall; page 127 © Tieghan Gerard; page 131 © Dev Amadeo; page 141 © Courtney Perry

CONTENTS

INTRODUCTION 6

CHAPTER 1: COOKIES 9

HOMEMADE OREOS
Joanne Chang, Flour Bakery 10

PLAIN JANE COOKIES
Amy Jason, Cookie Fix 12

BROWN BUTTER NUTELLA STUFFED
CHOCOLATE CHIP COOKIES
Chelsey White, *Chelsweets* 14

MADELEINES
Daniel Boulud, chef and restaurateur 16

ITALIAN SANDWICH COOKIES
Allison Robicelli, food writer and cookbook
author 21

OATMEAL CHOCOLATE TOFFEE
SHORTBREAD COOKIES
Clyde Greenhouse, Kessler Baking
Studio 22

FUNFETTI COOKIES
Kate Wood, *Wood & Spoon* 25

MACKLES'MORES
Robin Wehl Martin, Hello Robin Cookies 28

COOKIES AND CREAM MACARONS
Cambrea Gordon, *Cambrea Bakes* 30

CHOCOLATE PECAN CARAMEL COOKIES
Courtney Cowan, Milk Jar Cookies 33

SALTED PEANUT BUTTER COOKIES
Agatha Kulaga and Erin Patinkin, Ovenly 34

TRIPLE CHOCOLATE CHIP COOKIES
Camila Arango and Tom Wellings, Pluma by
Bluebird Bakery 37

CHAPTER 2: CAKES 39

BIRTHDAY LAYER CAKE
Christina Tosi, Milk Bar Bakery 40

ULTIMATE S'MORES CAKE
Courtney Rich, *Cake by Courtney* 43

STRAWBERRY CHAMPAGNE CUPCAKES
Sophie Kallinis LaMontagne and Katherine
Kallinis Berman, Georgetown Cupcake 48

RED VELVET LAYER CAKE
Tanya Holland, Brown Sugar Kitchen 53

DEATH BY CHOCOLATE CAKE
Liz Marek, *Sugar Geek Show* 54

LEMON LAYER CAKE WITH LEMON CURD
AND SUGARED BLUEBERRIES
Sugar Bakeshop 56

YUM YUM BANANA COFFEE CAKE WITH
CHEESECAKE FILLING AND CHOCOLATE
STREUSEL
Mindy Segal, Mindy's Bakery 62

DAYDREAM BELIEVER CUPCAKES
Kat Gordon, Muddy's Bake Shop 65

POUND CAKE
Stephanie Hart, Brown Sugar Bakery **66**

CHOCOLATE POUND CAKE WITH
CARAMEL ICING
Jocelyn Delk Adams, *Grandbaby Cakes* **68**

CARROT CAKE WITH CREAM CHEESE
FROSTING
Astrid Field, *The Sweet Rebellion* **71**

OLIVE OIL CAKE
Angela Renee Chase, Flora Bodega & Paseo
Farmers Market **72**

CHAPTER 3: PIES & TARTS **75**

STRAWBERRY HAND PIES
Tracy Wilk, *#BakeItForward* **76**

CLASSIC APPLE PIE
The Upper Crust Pie Bakery **79**

PASSION FRUIT PIE WITH MACADAMIA
LACE BRITTLE
Darcy Schein and Leslie Coale-Mossman,
Pie Junkie **80**

BLUEBERRY LEMON PIE (THE BOY SCOUT)
Shauna Lott Harman, The Long I
Pie Shop **83**

STRAWBERRY LABNEH GRANOLA TART
Majed Ali, *The Cinnaman* **84**

CHOCOLATE CARAMEL TART
Erica Leahy, Three Daughters Baking **88**

PEANUT BUTTER PIE
Kelli Marks, Sweet Love Bakes **91**

BLUEBERRY GALETTE
Jennifer Essex, Ruby Jean Patisserie **92**

CHAPTER 4: THINGS YOU EAT WITH YOUR HANDS **97**

CHEWY BROWNIES
Tessa Arias, *Handle the Heat* **99**

CHOCOLATE BABKA
Duff Goldman, Charm City Cakes **100**

CROISSANTS
Dominique Ansel, Dominique Ansel
Bakery **102**

LEMON BARS
Ashley Summers, Berkshire Bakes **107**

BLONDIE ATE A BROWNIE
Sherry Blockinger, Sherry B Dessert
Studio **110**

PISTACHIO CHEESECAKE BARS
Katina Talley, Sweet Magnolias Bake
Shop **113**

CHOCOLATE CHEESECAKE MOCHI MUFFINS
Sam Butarbutar, Third Culture Bakery **114**

SALTED CARAMEL BROWNIES
Kimberlee Ho, *Kickass Baker* **117**

PEACH COBBLER SCONES
Rebecca Rather, Emma + Ollie **118**

BISCOFF WHITE CHOCOLATE BLONDIES
Anna Wierzbinska, *Anna Banana* **121**

CHAPTER 5: THINGS YOU PROBABLY SHOULDN'T EAT WITH YOUR HANDS **125**

BROWN SUGAR PEACH COBBLER
Tieghan Gerard, *Half Baked Harvest* **126**

RHUBARB CHEESECAKE
Erin Jeanne McDowell, *The Fearless Baker* **129**

CREAMY COCONUT CHEESECAKE WITH DULCE DE LECHE
Dev Amadeo, *The Yellow Butterfly* **130**

BUTTER PECAN CINNAMON BUNS
Ashley Manila, *Baker by Nature* **132**

GRAPEFRUIT TIRAMISU
Anne Ng and Jeremy Mandrell, Bakery Lorraine **134**

CLASSIC CRÈME BRÛLÉE
Jeff Osaka, chef/restaurateur **137**

CHOCOLATE CROISSANT BREAD PUDDING WITH FRESH CHANTILLY CREAM
Wiltshire Pantry Bakery & Café **139**

CHOCOLATE SOUFFLÉS WITH CHOCOLATE SAUCE
Hedda Gioia Dowd and Cherif Brahmi, rise n°1 restaurant **140**

RECOMMENDED READING **142**

ACKNOWLEDGMENTS **143**

ABOUT THE AUTHOR **144**

INTRODUCTION

I know what you're thinking: What kind of morbid chick puts baking—the sweetest, the most sublime of life's pleasures—in the same sentence as death? Can't we just have our cake without being confronted with our ever-hastening mortality, too?

I get it. I, too, value baked goods and detest the fact that someday I will cease to exist. (And, therefore, taste.)

Which is exactly why this book is so critical. What if I took my last breath without experiencing the revelation that is Nutella stuffed into salty, brown-buttery, chocolate chip cookies? Would my life have been wasted had I not bit into the creamy coconut cheesecake with dulce de leche on page 130?

This collection of recipes—gifted to us from the greatest bakers and chefs, from small-town cafes to fancy restaurants to TV show hosts— is a call to arms, to action, to revolution! Or, at the very least, a call to turn on the oven.

This book is designed for baking mortals like myself. I cannot make a perfectly crimped pie crust, and my cakes don't look like works of art, or even works of a third grader. Some of the photos in this cookbook are of my creations, and others are from the creators of the recipes. You can most certainly tell the difference. The point of this book, though, isn't to make the most beautiful lemon layer cake but to make the tastiest, and that should be accessible to all levels of bakers.

Trust me when I say that if I can bake it, you can bake it. I'm not what you'd typically expect of a food writer—I have no formal cooking experience. (OK fine, I don't have much informal cooking experience either.) I am a food enthusiast, not an expert, but I like to think that my intense passion for eating makes up for my lack of skill in the kitchen. What I'm good at is making food fun; encouraging people to try new dishes and think about ingredients and restaurants differently.

In this cookbook, I hope to encourage you to try new things, too. Some of these recipes are easy and familiar, while others are super intimidating and will have you feeling like a superhero when you complete them. Bake them all! I mean, why not? It's not like your life is going to be worse for having a plate of fudgy brownies in front of you.

I've grouped the recipes into five categories— Cookies, Cakes, Pies/Tarts, Things You Eat with Your Hands, and Things You Probably Shouldn't Eat with Your Hands—because it seemed like that covered all of the dessert-y bases. I left out total recipe times because for one, they're never accurate. It takes me a whole lot longer than a pro baker to level a cake or figure out how to pipe a cookie, and there's nothing worse than false expectations. Take the time you need. And for another, it forces you to read the recipe all the way through before beginning so you know what to expect. Some recipes require doughs to rest for hours, or overnight. By reading the recipe's ingredients and steps before you start, you will be better prepared to rock it. (And to actually have that room temperature butter at room temperature!)

With our days and hours waning, it's our right as human beings to fully indulge in the very best desserts the sweet, sweet confectionary world has to offer. Because we don't have time for the third-best brownie recipe, or for the easiest chocolate soufflé.

Look. We're all on the clock here. We're all just spirits in a material world, or spiritual beings having a human experience, or whatever else the wise prophets Sting and Oprah told us about our lives. So why not be the beings who eat the red velvet cake to make the human experience a little more enjoyable?

All of this is to say that I encourage you to go for it. To bake with reckless abandon, no matter how many steps the recipe asks of you. Because life isn't measured by how many breaths you take, but by how many bites of Biscoff white chocolate blondies you take. So bake them.

✦ **Before You Die.** ✦

CHAPTER 1

Cookies

HOMEMADE OREOS 10
Joanne Chang, co-owner of Flour
Bakery in Boston, MA

PLAIN JANE COOKIES 12
Amy Jason, owner of Cookie Fix in Homewood, AL

**BROWN BUTTER NUTELLA
STUFFED CHOCOLATE
CHIP COOKIES 14**
Chelsey White, baking blogger and
content creator (*Chelsweets*)

MADELEINES 16
Daniel Boulud, chef and restaurateur

ITALIAN SANDWICH COOKIES 21
Allison Robicelli, food writer and cookbook author

**OATMEAL CHOCOLATE TOFFEE
SHORTBREAD COOKIES 22**
Clyde Greenhouse, owner of Kessler
Baking Studio in Dallas, TX

FUNFETTI COOKIES 25
Kate Wood, baking blogger (*Wood & Spoon*)

MACKLES'MORES 28
Robin Wehl Martin, owner of Hello
Robin Cookies in Seattle, WA

**COOKIES AND CREAM
MACARONS 30**
Cambrea Gordon, baking
blogger (*Cambrea Bakes*)

**CHOCOLATE PECAN
CARAMEL COOKIES 33**
Courtney Cowan, owner of Milk Jar
Cookies in Los Angeles, CA

**SALTED PEANUT BUTTER
COOKIES 34**
Agatha Kulaga and Erin Patinkin,
owners of Ovenly in New York, NY

**TRIPLE CHOCOLATE
CHIP COOKIES 37**
Camila Arango and Tom Wellings, Pluma
by Bluebird Bakery in Washington, DC

Homemade Oreos

Joanne Chang, co-owner of Flour Bakery in Boston, MA

Makes 16 to 18 sandwich cookies

For the cookies:

1 cup (2 sticks) unsalted butter, melted

¾ cup sugar

1 teaspoon vanilla extract

1 cup semisweet chocolate chips, melted

1 egg

1½ cups all-purpose flour

¾ cup Dutch-processed cocoa powder

½ teaspoon baking soda

1 teaspoon kosher salt

For the filling:

½ cup (1 stick) unsalted butter, softened

1 teaspoon vanilla extract

1⅔ cups confectioners' sugar

1 tablespoon milk

pinch of salt

Before Joanne Chang was a James Beard Award–winning baker, she was just another little girl dealing with the oppressive tyranny that is a mom denying her commercially-made treats. As is the case with many of us innocent victims of moms shutting down our greatest wishes, Joanne went on to become an adult who rebelled, creating her very own version of the cookie that eluded her as a child, the prized Oreo.

Her cookies are made with bittersweet cocoa powder and melted chocolate chips, and filled with sweetened butter. The outside is all deep chocolate business while the inside is a sticky sweet party. They're one of my kids' favorite cookies, and adults dig them, too.

Oh, and guess what? Even Joanne's mom loves them.

1. Combine the melted butter and sugar in a medium bowl and whisk until combined. Whisk in the vanilla and melted chocolate. Add the egg and whisk until combined.

2. Combine the flour, cocoa powder, baking soda, and salt in another medium bowl. Use a wooden spoon to stir the flour mixture into the chocolate mixture. (The dough will start to seem too floury—it's easiest to switch to mixing the dough with your hands until it comes together. It will have the consistency of Play-Doh.)

3. Let the dough sit for about an hour at room temperature to firm up. Place the dough on a 15-inch square sheet of parchment or waxed paper. Shape with your hands into a rough log shape, about 10 inches long and 2½ inches in diameter. Place the log at the edge of its sheet of parchment paper and roll the parchment around the log. With the log fully encased in parchment, roll it into a smoother log shape (still 2½ inches in diameter). Refrigerate

the log until firm, at least 2 hours. You may need to re-roll it every so often to maintain that nice, round shape, but it's not the end of the world if they're not perfect circles.

4. Heat the oven to 325°F. Remove the parchment from the dough log and slice the log into ¼-inch-thick slices. Place the slices about 1 inch apart on a cookie sheet lined with parchment paper or buttered and bake for 20 to 25 minutes, until firm to the touch. Check them frequently after 16 or 17 minutes and poke them in the middle. As soon as they feel firm to the touch remove from the oven. Let cool to warm or room temperature on the cookie sheet or a wire rack.

5. Meanwhile, make the vanilla cream filling. In the bowl of a stand mixer fitted with a paddle attachment (or with an electric hand mixer), mix the butter on low speed for about 30 seconds. Add the vanilla and the confectioners' sugar and mix until totally smooth. Add milk and pinch of

salt and continue to paddle until smooth. It will look like white spackle and feel about the same—like putty. Bring to room temperature before using.

6. Use a tablespoon to scoop out a rounded tablespoon of filling and place it between two cookies. Press the cookies together to distribute the filling toward the edges and serve. The cookies may be stored for up to 3 days at room temperature in an airtight container.

Plain Jane Cookies

Amy Jason, owner of Cookie Fix in Homewood, AL

2 cups (4 sticks) unsalted butter, slightly softened

6 ounces cream cheese, softened

2½ cups sugar

2 egg yolks

1 tablespoon vanilla

2⅔ cups flour

3⅓ cups oats

1 teaspoon salt

½ cup turbinado sugar for coating dough balls

Amy Jason is cookie obsessed, and while her cookie mania may cause her some inconvenient OCD flare-ups, it makes for incredibly delicious and unique cookies for the rest of us. These Plain Janes are anything but—chewy on the inside but crispy on the outside, this oatmeal-sugar cookie hybrid with a kick of cream cheese is unlike any cookie you've ever had. Yet they taste so familiar, so snuggly, so *cookie-y*, that they just might be what you think of from now on when you hear the word "cookie." It's no wonder they've developed an impassioned following at Cookie Fix.

Jane's base is versatile, and while these are perfectly delightful as is, you can deck them out with your favorite mix-ins. Amy loves them with blueberries, white chocolate chips, walnuts, and a little lemon zest, and if you think that you, too, might love them that way, add ½ cup each of the white chocolate and walnuts, ¾ cup blueberries, and the zest of a lemon to the dough before chilling. Consider yourself Plain Jane cookie obsessed.

1. Beat the butter, cream cheese, and sugar at medium speed with an electric mixer until creamy. A wooden spoon may be used, but the batter will be thick and hard to stir. Add the egg yolks and vanilla, beating until well blended.

2. Combine the flour, oats, and salt in a small bowl. Gradually add the flour mixture to the butter and sugar mixture, beating until blended and scraping the sides of the bowl occasionally. If you want to add any mix-ins, this is the time to do it. Chill the dough in the refrigerator for about 30 minutes to make the dough more firm and easier to scoop.

3. Using a cookie scoop, scoop dough into 2½-ounce balls (slightly smaller than a golf ball), keeping the exterior texture of the dough ball rough, not smoothed with your hands. This gives the cookies more texture and creates a crispy exterior. Freeze dough balls on any baking sheet or pan that will fit in your freezer. When firm, place in a freezer zipper bag and store in the freezer until ready to bake. For best results, let dough balls freeze at least overnight for flavors to meld.

4. When ready to bake, preheat the oven to 375°F. Toss the frozen dough balls in turbinado sugar in the ziploc bag used for storage. Place frozen dough balls on an ungreased baking sheet, at least 4 inches apart. Bake for 8 minutes; rotate the pan 180 degrees and bake for another 6 to 8 minutes until slightly golden. For a crisper cookie, bake an additional 2 to 4 minutes. (Cookies will spread more if you bake longer.) Let cool to set. Cookies will be gooey for 1 to 2 hours after baking. When completely cool, store between wax sheets in an airtight container.

Brown Butter Nutella Stuffed Chocolate Chip Cookies

Chelsey White, baking blogger and content creator (*Chelsweets*)

Makes one dozen

½ cup (1 stick) unsalted butter

¾ cup Nutella

¾ cup packed light or dark brown sugar

1 large egg, room temperature

½ teaspoon vanilla extract

2 teaspoons sour cream or plain Greek yogurt

1¼ cups all-purpose flour

⅔ teaspoon baking soda

½ teaspoon salt

1 cup dark or milk chocolate chips or chunks

coarse sea salt

Nothing is better than these cookies. Nothing. They are better than the day you got married, better than the day your first child was born, better than the day you realized your life's calling. You know why? Because Nutella, brown butter, and chocolate chunks are better than those things. They just are.

These cookies are perfection. My only tip is to double the recipe because I can't imagine only wanting to eat 12 of these.

1. Begin by browning the butter. Melt butter in a saucepan over medium heat until it begins to foam. Make sure you stir and scrape the sides and bottom of the pan frequently with a rubber spatula. After a couple of minutes, the butter will begin to brown; continue to stir and remove from heat as soon as the butter is visibly brown and gives off a nutty aroma. Immediately transfer the butter to a separate heatproof bowl and cool in the fridge for 30 minutes.

2. While the brown butter cools, prepare the Nutella centers. Line a cookie sheet with parchment paper, and use two spoons to create 12 equal-sized scoops of Nutella, using about 1 tablespoon of Nutella per scoop. This is the hardest part of the recipe—getting the sticky Nutella into neatish globs. You will probably have to lick a lot of it off your fingers as you're globbing. Whatever it takes, intrepid baker. Whatever it takes. Place this pan in the freezer to allow them to firm up.

3. With a hand or stand mixer, cream together the cooled brown butter and brown sugar for 2 to 3 minutes, until

the mixture lightens in color. Use a rubber spatula to scrape the sides and bottom of the bowl as needed. Mix in the egg, vanilla extract, and sour cream or Greek yogurt on medium-high speed until the mixture is smooth. Add in the flour, baking soda, and salt. Mix on low speed just until combined—you do not want to overmix your dough. Gently fold in the chocolate.

4. The dough should be a bit sticky at this point. Chill the cookie dough for 30 to 60 minutes, until it's thicker and easier to handle. About 20 minutes before your cookies are done chilling, preheat the oven to 350°F.

5. Use a cookie scoop to make 12 equal-sized cookie dough balls. Remove the Nutella from the freezer. Flatten each ball of cookie dough in the palm of your hand, and place a frozen scoop of Nutella in the center. Fold the dough around the Nutella and shape into a hockey puck, making sure the Nutella is fully covered. Set aside and repeat with the remaining cookie dough.

6. Line two baking sheets with parchment paper, aluminum foil, or a silicone baking mat. Place the cookie dough balls 2 to 3 inches apart on the prepared cookie sheets. Top with a few extra bits of chocolate if desired. Bake the cookies for 9 to 10 minutes, until the edges just begin to brown. Rotate the pans halfway through to help the cookies bake evenly. Remove them from the oven and garnish with sea salt while they're still hot. Let the cookies cool on the pan for 15 minutes, then move to a wire rack to finish cooling.

Madeleines

Daniel Boulud, chef and restaurateur

Makes one dozen large or six dozen mini madeleines

¾ cup all-purpose flour

1 teaspoon baking powder

pinch of salt

¼ cup plus 2 tablespoons granulated sugar

2 large eggs

1 tablespoon honey

1 tablespoon packed light brown sugar

finely grated zest of 1 lemon

6 tablespoons unsalted butter, melted and kept warm

confectioners' sugar, for dusting

Special equipment:

madeleine pan

Madeleines are not a flashy, American-style cookie. There's no chocolate or peanut butter or crunchy bits or whatever else you dig up in your pantry inside of them. I know this is strange for us, but let's hear the madeleines out.

Madeleines are a classic French cookie/cake, typically made in a delicate, slightly lemon-y flavor. This recipe comes to us courtesy of Daniel Boulud, and who are we to argue with freaking Daniel Boulud about the flashiness of a cookie/cake? No one, that's who, so we're going to make the madeleines just as God and Boulud intended.

Now that we've gotten what madeleines *aren't* out of the way, let's talk a little bit more about what they *are*. The outside is crispy, like a cookie, while the inside is spongy, like a cake. These have a hint of lemon to them and are topped with confectioners' sugar, but they can also be made with ground almonds and topped with jam. Madeleines are nuanced, refined, and just making them will increase your classiness by about 25 percent. When I made them, I swear I sprouted opera gloves and a monocle.

To get the telltale scallop-shell design, you're going to need a special madeleine pan. I got one on Amazon for pretty cheap, and specialty baking gear shops should carry them, too. For this recipe you will also need a pastry bag and tip, but since I didn't have those on-hand, I poured the batter into a Ziploc baggie and cut a slice off a corner to pipe the batter into the pan. Worked like a charm.

Now sure, you could go get these at Restaurant Daniel, but first you'll have to shell out—it's a madeleine joke; you wouldn't get it—upwards of $200 for the tasting menu, so it might be worth it to try these at home.

---

1. In a small bowl, sift together the flour, baking powder, and salt. Set aside.

2. In a medium bowl using a wire whisk, mix the granulated sugar, eggs, honey, brown sugar, and lemon zest. Add the flour mixture and whisk just until combined. Add the melted butter, stirring just until incorporated. Cover the bowl with plastic wrap and refrigerate for 1 hour and up to 24 hours for best results.

3. Preheat the oven to 400°F. Liberally spray a 12-mold madeleine pan with nonstick cooking spray.

4. Place the batter in a pastry bag fitted with a medium round tip. Pipe the molds two-thirds full, using about 2 tablespoons of batter.

5. Bake for 5 minutes, reduce the heat to 350°F, rotate the pan, and continue baking until the centers rise and the edges are golden brown, about 5 minutes. Remove from the oven, invert the pan, and tap it against the counter to release the madeleines. Serve the madeleines warm, dusted with confectioners' sugar.

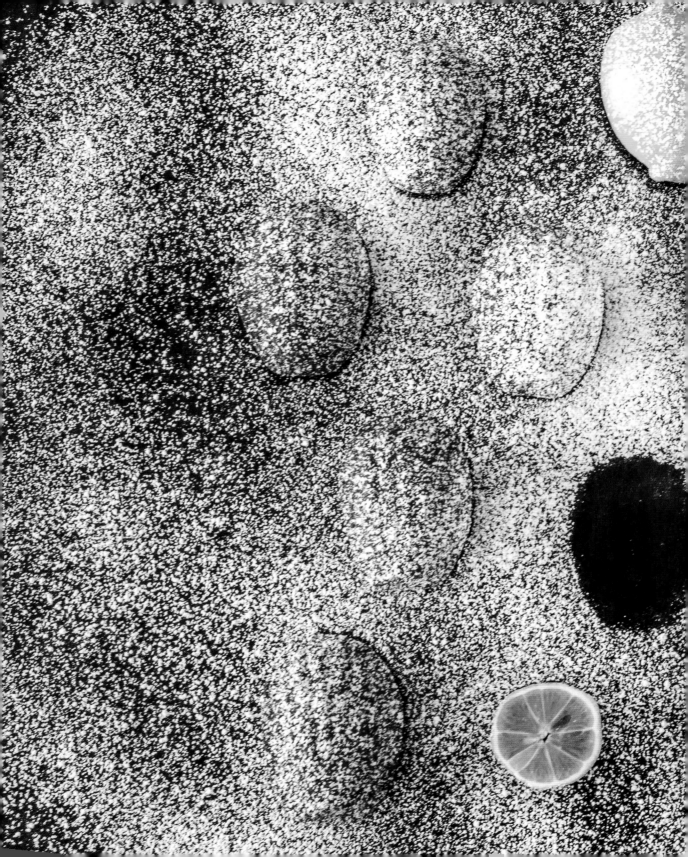

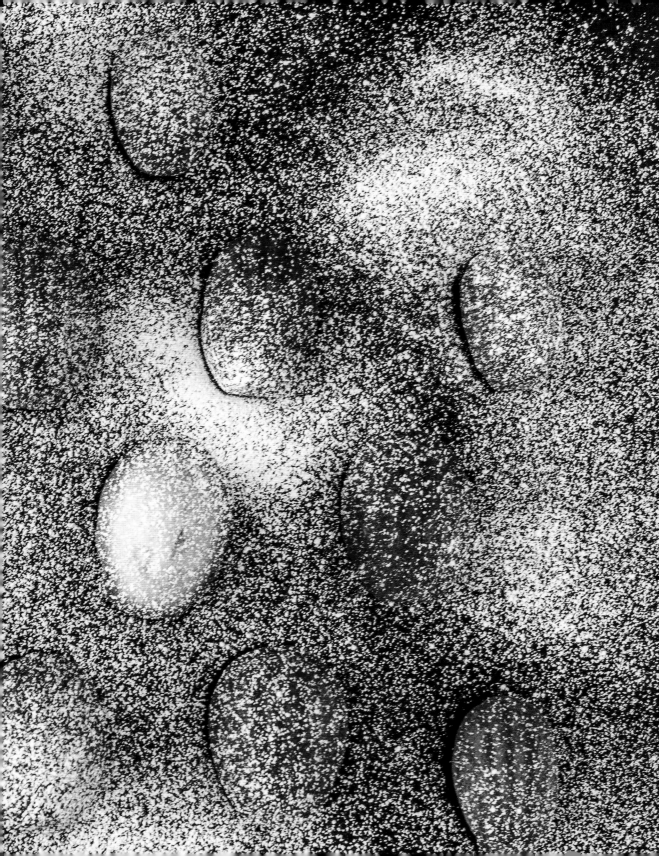

Italian Sandwich Cookies

Allison Robicelli, food writer and cookbook author

Makes two dozen cookies

1½ cups (3 sticks) unsalted butter, room temperature

1½ cups sugar

1 teaspoon kosher salt

1 teaspoon vanilla extract

2 large eggs

3½ cups all-purpose flour

1 teaspoon baking powder

1 cup raspberry jam

¾ cup chopped chocolate or chocolate chips

1 teaspoon canola oil or shortening

rainbow sprinkles, for decorating

Special equipment:

pastry bag or cookie press fitted with a star tip

The first time I learned about Allison Robicelli was via an Instagram post: "I got censored for writing about frat boys chugging limoncello through ass funnels, yet Fifty Shades is allowed to sell ALL SORTS of butt stuff at Costco. I get that I wrote a cupcake cookbook, but still."

Needless to say, I was in love.

You will probably like Allison Robicelli, too. Or at the very least, you will use her for her baked goods, which is totally fine.

These Italian sandwich cookies are a riff on classic spritz cookies brought over by Italian immigrants. Not only are they super tasty—and super buttery, but that's the same thing—but they're coated in chocolate and sprinkles. Because once you're three sticks of butter in (seriously, three sticks), what's some chocolate and sprinkles?

1. In a mixer on medium speed, cream together the butter, sugar, and salt until very fluffy, about 4 minutes. Add the vanilla and eggs and continue to beat very well for an additional 4 minutes, scraping down the sides at least once. Turn the mixer on low speed and add the flour and baking powder, and mix until just combined.

2. Put the dough into a pastry bag or cookie press fitted with a star tip. On an ungreased cookie sheet, pipe cookies in 2-inch lines, spaced at least 1 inch apart. If the tip just isn't working, ditch it and pipe directly from the slit bag. The only difference is that the cookies will look more like milanos, and that's not so bad. The dough will pipe easier if it's warmed to room temperature a bit, so no rush here. Meanwhile, preheat the oven to 375°F. Place the piped cookies in the freezer for 5 to 10 minutes. (This will help them retain their shape while baking.)

3. Bake until golden brown, 15 minutes. Let cool on the cookie sheets 3 minutes, then transfer to wire racks to cool completely. Spread a little more than half a teaspoon of jam on half of the cookies, then top with the remaining cookies to make sandwiches. Place in the freezer for another 5 minutes to help set while you prepare the chocolate.

4. Toss together the chocolate and the oil and place in a microwave-safe mug. Microwave in 30-second increments, stirring occasionally, until completely melted. Put the rainbow sprinkles onto a plate.

5. Working quickly, dip the cookies halfway into the chocolate, then roll in the sprinkles. Place finished cookies on a tray lined with either wax or parchment paper to set completely.

Oatmeal Chocolate Toffee Shortbread Cookies

Clyde Greenhouse, owner of Kessler Baking Studio in Dallas, TX

*Makes 36 4-inch cookies
or 72 2-inch cookies*

1 cup rolled oats

2 cups granulated sugar

2 cups (4 sticks) unsalted butter, room temperature

1 large egg

1 tablespoon vanilla extract

3¾ cups all-purpose flour

1 teaspoon kosher salt

1 cup mini semisweet chocolate chips

½ cup toffee bits

There's a time and a place for ooey gooey, but it's not in a shortbread, and it's not when toffee is involved. Clyde Greenhouse, known as the bow-tie baker in Dallas because of his dapper choice of baking wear, originally created these shortbread cookies as favors for his niece's wedding. This is good because 1) The only acceptable type of wedding favors are edible ones, and 2) We get to eat these cookies, even though we weren't invited to the wedding.

These cookies really speak to those of us who want their baked goods to put up a bit of a fight. I like my cookies with a crunch, not to roll over and acquiesce quite so easily. If you do too, you will love these chocolate chip- and toffee-studded shortbreads. The toffee gives them a little something extra, but if you're having trouble finding toffee, a cut-up Heath bar works fine.

1. In a food processor, grind rolled oats to a mealy consistency.

2. Cream sugar and butter in a stand mixer fitted with the paddle attachment on medium speed. Use spatula to scrape down the bowl as needed and continue mixing until there are no visible butter pieces. Add egg and vanilla extract and mix until completely incorporated. Scrape down the bowl as needed.

3. In a large bowl, whisk together flour, ground oats, and salt. With mixer on low speed, add dry ingredients to butter mixture in thirds and mix until crumbly in texture. Add semisweet chocolate chips and toffee bits and mix until dough comes away from the bowl and begins to cling to the paddle.

4. Turn dough out onto plastic wrap and form into a disk. Chill wrapped dough for at least 4 hours, or overnight for best results.

5. The next day, cut disk into wedges. Using a rolling pin and on a smooth, lightly floured surface, roll dough out to ¼-inch thickness and cut into desired shape. Place cut-outs onto a parchment-lined baking sheet and refrigerate for at least 10 minutes while preheating the oven to 350°F. Bake 4-inch cookies 16 to 18 minutes, or 2-inch cookies 12 to 14 minutes, until edges are lightly browned.

Funfetti Cookies

Kate Wood, baking blogger (*Wood & Spoon*)

Makes about 30 cookies

10 tablespoons (1¼ sticks) unsalted butter, room temperature

1 cup sugar

½ cup brown sugar

2½ teaspoons clear vanilla

1 large egg

2 cups all-purpose flour

1 teaspoon baking soda

¾ teaspoon salt

½ teaspoon cream of tartar

1 cup rainbow sprinkles

I anger-baked these funfetti cookies. That may seem like an odd choice for an anger bake, but hear me out. There were all levels of drama going on at my house, including, but not limited to, refereeing kid fights over snow shovels and hammers. It was either anger-bake or pack a bag and head for the airport. But since my kids need a mother, I chose the funfetti. In return, I got to play with rainbow sprinkles, had a house smelling of vanilla, and achieved (temporary) household peace as my kids set aside their hammer differences to help pour in ingredients.

So yes, I recommend anger-baking Kate Wood's funfetti cookies, which taste like buttery nostalgia. They lead to happy eating, because sugar and rainbow sprinkles are known for their anger-melting properties.

1. Preheat the oven to 350°F. Prepare baking sheets by lining them with silicone mats or parchment paper.

2. In a large mixing bowl or the bowl of a stand mixer, cream the butter, sugar, and brown sugar on medium speed until light and fluffy, about 2 minutes. Scrape the sides of the bowl and add the vanilla and egg, beating on low until incorporated.

3. Add the flour, baking soda, salt, and cream of tartar and beat on low speed until the dry ingredients are just combined. Scrape the sides of the bowl and add the sprinkles. Beat until just combined.

4. Scoop out 1 to 1½ tablespoon sized scoops and roll each dough ball briefly in your hands to smooth out the edges. Place on prepared baking sheets 2 inches apart. Bake for about 10 minutes, or until the tops of the cookies have just begun to crack and the edges are set. Allow to cool for about 5 minutes before transferring to a rack to complete cooling.

Mackles'mores

Robin Wehl Martin, owner of Hello Robin Cookies in Seattle, WA

Makes 36 cookies

2¾ cups all-purpose flour

1 teaspoon ground cinnamon

1 teaspoon kosher salt

1 teaspoon baking soda

¾ cup (1½ sticks) unsalted butter

1 cup packed light brown sugar

½ cup granulated sugar

2 large eggs

1 teaspoon vanilla extract

4 ounces dark chocolate (70%), cut into chunks, or chips

1 cup packed mini marshmallows

36 graham cracker squares

7½ ounces milk chocolate squares (I broke up some Hershey's bars)

Was it a love for everyone's favorite campfire treat or a love for socially conscious hip-hop that inspired Robin Wehl Martin to create this special cookie? While we may never know the depths of Robin's affection for thrift shopping, we can know the deliciousness of her Mackles'mores cookies, which are bursting with melted chocolate and mini marshmallows. Eat them warm and toasty, like you would a traditional s'more.

1. Line two baking sheets with parchment paper and set aside. Whisk together the flour, cinnamon, salt, and baking soda in a medium bowl; set aside.

2. Cream the butter, brown sugar, and granulated sugar in a stand mixer on medium-high speed until pale and fluffy, about 3 minutes. Add the eggs one at a time, mixing on medium speed for 15 seconds after each addition. Add the vanilla and mix until smooth.

3. Add the dry ingredients and mix until combined. Fold in the dark chocolate and marshmallows.

4. Using a medium cookie scoop (about 1½ tablespoons), scoop the dough into balls and place them on one of the prepared baking sheets. Freeze for at least an hour.

5. Preheat the oven to 400°F. Place the graham crackers side by side on the second prepared baking sheet. Place 1 ball of the frozen cookie dough on each graham cracker. Bake until the cookies are puffed and just turning golden, 10 to 12 minutes. Remove the baking sheet from the oven and immediately press 1 piece of milk chocolate onto each hot cookie—don't be afraid to really squish it down so that when it melts, it puddles on the cookie and doesn't run off.

Cookies and Cream Macarons

Cambrea Gordon, baking blogger (*Cambrea Bakes*)

Makes 18 to 20 macarons

For the chocolate cookie crumb:

3 tablespoons butter

½ cup all-purpose flour

1 teaspoon cornstarch

⅛ teaspoon salt

2 tablespoons granulated sugar

¼ cup cocoa powder

For the macaron shells:

1⅔ cups blanched almond meal (or almond flour)

1¼ cups powdered sugar

½ cup granulated sugar

3 large egg whites, room temperature

¼ teaspoon cream of tartar

3 drops gel black food coloring

For the cookies and cream buttercream:

10 tablespoons (1¼ sticks) butter, room temperature

1 cup powdered sugar

½ tablespoon milk

½ to ⅔ cup chocolate cookie crumb

I think we can all agree that macarons are the cutest cookies. They're so irresistibly adorable that I just want to squish them, crushing them with the weight of my love. That's not great, though, because that's messy and throws off the texture, so we should resist pinching them until they burst.

My issue with macarons can be with the taste. They're never bad—I'm not kicking macarons out of bed or anything—but the taste doesn't typically live up to their super-cute appearance. (What could? They're freaking adorable!) Cambrea Gordon's cookies and cream macarons somehow taste just as dazzling as they look, and that's saying something because look at that dazzle. Although macarons seem intimidating to make, they're actually easier than I thought. And if I can produce a totes adorbs little cookie sandwich, then anyone can.

---

1. Preheat the oven to 300°F. For the chocolate cookie crumb: In a small bowl, melt the butter. In a separate medium bowl, combine the flour, cornstarch, sugar, salt, and cocoa powder. Pour in melted butter and mix until it comes together and forms a crumb.

2. Line a baking sheet with parchment paper, and pour crumb onto sheet. Bake for 20 minutes. Allow crumb to cool completely before using.

3. For the shells: Sift the almond meal and powdered sugar together in a large bowl. Set aside.

4. Add egg whites to stand mixing bowl with whisk attachment and whip on medium speed for 1 minute, until foamy. Add cream of tartar. Sprinkle in the granulated sugar, not too much at a time or it will deflate the egg whites. After sugar is added, increase speed to medium-high for 5 to 6 minutes. Add black food coloring and whip on

medium high for 1 to 2 minutes, until whites hold a stiff peak.

5. Add the whipped egg whites to a large bowl. Add ⅓ of the almond meal/sugar mixture to the whites. Fold gently with a spatula until combined. Add the next ⅓ and fold to combine. Continue until all dry ingredients are incorporated. Using a rubber spatula, scrape the batter against the side of the bowl. Every few scrapes, pick up the batter and let it fall into the bowl. The batter should flow slowly in ribbons. Try to make a figure eight with the batter. If it falls without breaking, it's ready.

6. Flip a baking pan upside down and line it with parchment paper or silicone baking mat. Fill a piping bag fitted with a small round tip with the batter. Pipe your little circles directly over the top of the parchment. When the pan is full, rap and drop the pan on the counter to release any air bubbles. You can use a toothpick to pop any bubbles that come to the surface. Sprinkle tops of the shells with some of the chocolate cookie crumb.

7. Allow the macarons to sit out and form a skin. This can take anywhere from 30 minutes to an hour, depending on humidity. They're ready to bake when the shell can be touched without sticking to your finger or leaving an impression. Bake at 300°F for 13 to 14 minutes. They're done when you gently

touch the top of the shell and it just barely budges from the foot. Cool completely before filling.

8. For the buttercream: In a mixing bowl fitted with the paddle attachment, whip the butter on low speed for 1 to 2 minutes until smooth. Stop the mixer and add ½ cup of powdered sugar. Mix on low until combined. Add next ½ cup of sugar and mix on medium speed until very

white and fluffy, about 2 to 3 minutes. Add milk and mix to combine. Stop the mixer and add cookie crumb. Mix on low until just combined.

9. To assemble: Find equal matches for your shells. Flip one over and pipe a dollop of cookies and cream buttercream onto the center. Sandwich the cream with the other half of the shell. Let them sit in the fridge overnight for best results.

Chocolate Pecan Caramel Cookies

Courtney Cowan, owner of Milk Jar Cookies in Los Angeles, CA

Makes 15 to 18 3-inch cookies

3½ cups all-purpose flour

⅓ cup natural unsweetened cocoa powder

1 teaspoon baking soda

1 teaspoon table salt

11 tablespoons (⅔ cup) unsalted butter, cold and cubed

11 tablespoons (⅔ cup) shortening, room temperature

1 cup sugar

1 cup packed light brown sugar

2 extra large eggs, cold

1½ teaspoons pure vanilla extract

1½ cups pecan pieces

Rolo candies, halved (approximately 36 Rolos)

There's practically no dessert that ooey gooey caramel wouldn't improve, and chocolate cookies—flecked with sweet, buttery pecans no less—are no exception. For that killer caramel pull, Courtney Cowan both stuffs and tops these stunners with Rolo candies, meaning that molten chocolate-caramel excellence can, with careful nibbling strategy, be had with each bite. Eat these uber-thick, chewy cookies warm for peak gooiness.

1. Preheat the oven to 350°F. In a medium bowl, combine the flour, cocoa powder, baking soda, and salt. Set aside.

2. In a large mixing bowl or the bowl of a stand mixer, combine butter, shortening, sugar, brown sugar, eggs, and vanilla extract and beat on medium-low speed until combined with small chunks of butter remaining, approximately 30 seconds. Every time you mix ingredients, scrape down the sides of bowl with a spatula to be sure all ingredients are included in the mix—every bit matters!

3. Add half of the dry ingredient mixture and mix on low speed until just incorporated and no flour is visible, about 30 seconds. Add half of the remaining dry ingredients, mixing on low speed until flour is incorporated and all butter chunks are gone, approximately 20 seconds. Add remaining dry ingredients and mix until dough pulls away from the sides of the bowl and is not sticky to the touch, another 20 seconds. Be careful not to overmix—that's how you get flat cookies. Mix in pecans.

4. Line two baking sheets with parchment paper. Scooping the dough ⅓ cup at a time, place 2 Rolo halves in the middle and firmly roll into round balls approximately 1½ inches in diameter. With the dough ball still in your hands, top each cookie with 2 more Rolo halves, gently pushing them in to keep them in position while they bake. Place 6 cookies on each prepared baking sheet, spacing them out well, and put in oven on the middle and lower racks. Bake until the caramel candies are melted and you notice hairline cracks forming on the sides, approximately 12 to 14 minutes, spinning each tray 180 degrees and swapping their positions halfway through.

5. Let the cookies cool on the baking sheets for 10 minutes, then use a wide spatula to transfer them to a wire rack or parchment paper on the counter to cool completely. Let baking sheets cool before repeating with remaining dough.

© *Milk Jar Cookies Bakebook*, Welcome Books, and imprint of Rizzoli International Publications, Inc.

Salted Peanut Butter Cookies

Agatha Kulaga and Erin Patinkin, owners of Ovenly in New York, NY

*Makes 12 large cookies
or 24 small cookies*

**1¾ cups packed light
brown sugar**

2 large eggs, room temperature

½ teaspoon vanilla extract

**1¾ cups smooth peanut butter
("While the all-natural stuff
works just fine, Skippy is our
peanut butter brand of choice
for this recipe, as we've found it
retains the dough shape best.")**

coarse-grained sea salt, to finish

We all eat peanut butter straight from the jar, right? Plunging a spoon (or finger) into a fresh jar of Skippy is basically an inalienable human right, one that unites us all in sticky, peanut-buttery freedom. This recipe from New York City's sugar fiend–favorite bakery Ovenly celebrates that passion for PB with a recipe that places it front and center. These naturally gluten-free, five-ingredient cookies simultaneously flatter both your sweet and your salty tooth, and once you try them, you'll see why they're one of the bakery's best sellers.

1. Preheat the oven to 350°F. Line a rimmed sheet pan with parchment paper.

2. In a medium bowl, vigorously whisk together the light brown sugar and eggs until incorporated. Whisk in the vanilla extract. Add the peanut butter and mix with a spatula until smooth and completely incorporated and no ribbons of peanut butter can be seen. You know the dough is ready when it has the consistency of Play-Doh.

3. Using a scoop or a spoon, form the dough into 12 approximately 2-inch (2- to 2¼-ounce) balls and place them on the prepared rimmed sheet pan. For smaller cookies, use a heaping tablespoon.

4. Sprinkle the dough balls lightly with coarse-grained sea salt just before baking. (You can bake these cookies as soon as the dough is prepared, but they will retain their shape better if you freeze them for 15 minutes before baking.) Bake large cookies for 20 to 22 minutes, turning the rimmed sheet pan once halfway through baking. For smaller cookies, bake for 16 to 18 minutes. When finished, the cookies will be lightly golden and cracked on top. Let cool completely before serving.

Triple Chocolate Chip Cookies

Camila Arango and Tom Wellings, Pluma by Bluebird Bakery in Washington, DC

Makes 30 cookies

1⅓ cups (2 sticks + 2 tablespoons) butter

⅞ cup sugar

1 cup + 1 tablespoon light brown sugar

3 cups all-purpose flour

1⅓ teaspoons salt

1¾ teaspoons baking soda

2 eggs

1 teaspoon vanilla paste

1 cup semisweet chocolate chips

1 cup gianduja chunks (Camila and Tom like Amedei or Callabeut brands)

½ cup Valrhona Dulcey chocolate

Obviously pizza is humankind's greatest contribution to the world, but these cookies might be a close second. It takes some sourcing to get all three forms of chocolate for these cookies, but trust me that you will want them exactly as prescribed by Camila and Tom. The all-star is the gianduja, and if you haven't had gianduja, think of it as the OG Nutella, but better. It's like the Beyonce of the chocolate/hazelnut world, and it will melt on your tongue and stay in your heart forever. You will instantly become a gianduja evangelist and will probably look for gianduja fan clubs and may even get a gianduja tattoo. That would be totally understandable; even commendable.

For this recipe, you'll want the pliable little bars of gianduja (not a spread), which you should be able to find at specialty grocery stores or online.

1. Preheat the oven to 350°F. In a stand mixer or using a handheld, cream the butter and sugars until light and fluffy, 1 to 2 minutes. Scrape down sides of the bowl.

2. In a separate bowl, mix the flour, salt, and baking soda. Set aside.

3. Add eggs one at a time to the butter/sugar mixture, mixing in between and scraping down the bowl. Mix in vanilla. Add dry ingredients in two additions, barely mixing in between. Scrape between additions, careful to not overmix.

4. Add all three chocolates and stir by hand until just incorporated.

5. Scoop the dough onto an ungreased cookie sheet. (Mine were about ping pong ball–sized.) Bake 7 minutes, then rotate sheet and bake for another 7 to 8 minutes.

CHAPTER 2

Cakes

BIRTHDAY LAYER CAKE 40
Christina Tosi, Milk Bar Bakery

ULTIMATE S'MORES CAKE 43
Courtney Rich, baking blogger (*Cake by Courtney*)

**STRAWBERRY CHAMPAGNE
CUPCAKES 48**
Sophie Kallinis LaMontagne and Katherine Kallinis
Berman, cofounders of Georgetown Cupcake

RED VELVET LAYER CAKE 53
Tanya Holland, owner of Brown
Sugar Kitchen in Oakland, CA

DEATH BY CHOCOLATE CAKE 54
Liz Marek, baking blogger (*Sugar Geek Show*)

**LEMON LAYER CAKE WITH
LEMON CURD AND SUGARED
BLUEBERRIES 56**
Sugar Bakeshop in Charleston, SC

**YUM YUM BANANA COFFEE CAKE
WITH CHEESECAKE FILLING AND
CHOCOLATE STREUSEL 62**
Mindy Segal, owner of Mindy's
Bakery in Chicago, IL

**DAYDREAM BELIEVER
CUPCAKES 65**
Kat Gordon, owner of Muddy's
Bake Shop in Memphis, TN

POUND CAKE 66
Stephanie Hart, founder of Brown
Sugar Bakery, Chicago, IL

**CHOCOLATE POUND CAKE
WITH CARAMEL ICING 68**
Jocelyn Delk Adams, baking
blogger (*Grandbaby Cakes*)

**CARROT CAKE WITH CREAM
CHEESE FROSTING 71**
Astrid Field, baking blogger (*The Sweet Rebellion*)

OLIVE OIL CAKE 72
Angela Renee Chase, co-owner of Flora Bodega
& Paseo Farmers Market in Oklahoma City, OK

Birthday Layer Cake

Christina Tosi, Milk Bar Bakery

Makes one three-layer 6-inch cake

For the cake:

4 tablespoons (½ stick) butter, room temperature

⅓ cup vegetable shortening

1¼ cups granulated sugar

3 tablespoons tightly packed light brown sugar

3 eggs

½ cup buttermilk

⅓ cup grapeseed oil

2 teaspoons clear vanilla extract

2 cups cake flour

1½ teaspoons baking powder

¾ teaspoon kosher salt

¼ cup + 2 tablespoons rainbow sprinkles (divided)

For the cake crumb:

½ cup granulated sugar

1½ tablespoons tightly packed light brown sugar

¾ cup cake flour

½ teaspoon baking powder

½ teaspoon kosher salt

2 tablespoons rainbow sprinkles

¼ cup grapeseed oil

1 tablespoon clear vanilla extract

For the cake soak:

¼ cup milk

1 teaspoon clear vanilla extract

I feel like this should be called an unbirthday cake, because you shouldn't have to wait 365 days to attack this chipper tower of sprinkles, frosting, and vanilla cake. (And God forbid it's a leap year!) The recipe comes from perky pastry goddess Christina Tosi, so you know that it's going to be a. amazing and b. just plain fun.

Yes, there's a lot to this cake chock-full of glee, but come on, anything this chock-full of glee is going to require a little effort. If you take it step-by-step, one element at a time, it will come together better than you think—and you'll definitely be making it more than once a year.

1. For the cake: Preheat the oven to 350°F. Spray a quarter sheet pan (10x15 jelly roll pan) and line with parchment. Combine the butter, shortening, and sugars in the bowl of a stand mixer fitted with the paddle attachment and cream together on medium-high for 2 to 3 minutes.

2. Scrape down the sides of the bowl, add the eggs, and mix on medium-high for 2 to 3 minutes. Scrape down the sides of the bowl once more, and on low speed stream in the buttermilk, oil, and vanilla.

3. Increase the mixer speed to medium-high and paddle for 4 to 6 minutes, until the mixture is practically white, twice the size of your original fluffy butter-and-sugar mixture, and completely homogenous. Don't rush the process. You're basically forcing too much liquid into an already fatty mixture that doesn't want to make room for that liquid. There should be no streaks of fat or liquid. Stop the mixer and scrape down the sides of the bowl.

4. On very low speed, add the cake flour, baking powder, salt, and the ¼ cup rainbow sprinkles. Mix for 45 to 60 seconds, just until your batter comes together. Scrape down the sides of the bowl.

5. Using a spatula, spread the cake batter in an even layer in the quarter sheet pan. Sprinkle the remaining 2 tablespoons rainbow sprinkles evenly on top of the batter.

6. Bake the cake for 30 to 35 minutes. The cake will rise and puff, doubling in size, but will remain slightly buttery and dense. At 30 minutes, gently poke the edge of the cake with your finger—the cake should bounce back slightly, and the center should no longer be jiggly. Leave the cake in the oven for an extra 3 to 5 minutes if it doesn't pass these tests. Once it does, take the cake out of the oven and cool on a wire rack or, in a pinch, in the fridge or freezer. (Don't worry, it's not cheating!) The cooled cake can be stored in the fridge, wrapped in plastic wrap, for up to 5 days.

For the frosting:

8 tablespoons (1 stick) butter, room temperature

¼ cup vegetable shortening

2 ounces cream cheese

1 tablespoon glucose

1 tablespoon corn syrup

1 tablespoon clear vanilla extract

1¼ cups confectioners' sugar

½ teaspoon kosher salt

1 pinch baking powder

1 pinch citric acid

Special equipment:

6-inch cake ring

2 strips acetate, each 3 inches wide and 20 inches long

7. For the birthday cake crumb: Preheat the oven to 300°F. Line a baking sheet with parchment. Combine the sugars, flour, baking powder, salt, and sprinkles in the bowl of a stand mixer fitted with the paddle attachment and mix on low speed until well combined.

8. Add the oil and vanilla and paddle again to distribute. The wet ingredients will act as glue to help the dry ingredients form small clusters; continue paddling until that happens. Put on prepared baking sheet and bake for 15 minutes. Let the crumbs cool completely before using or scarfing by the handful. Stored in an airtight container, the crumbs will keep fresh for 1 week at room temperature or 1 month in the fridge or freezer.

9. For the cake soak: whisk together milk and vanilla in a small bowl.

10. For the frosting: Combine the butter, shortening, and cream cheese in the bowl of a stand mixer fitted with the paddle attachment and cream together on medium-high for 2 to 3 minutes, until the mixture is smooth and fluffy. Scrape down the sides of the bowl.

11. With the mixer on its lowest speed, stream in the glucose, corn syrup, and vanilla. Crank the mixer up to medium-high and beat for 2 to 3 minutes, until the mixture is silky smooth and a glossy white. Scrape down the sides of the bowl.

12. Add the confectioners' sugar, salt, baking powder, and citric acid and mix on low speed just to incorporate them into the batter. Crank the speed back up to medium-high and beat for 2 to 3 minutes, until you have a brilliant

stark white, beautifully smooth frosting. It should look just like it came out of a plastic tub at the grocery store! Use the frosting immediately, or store it in an airtight container in the fridge for up to 1 week.

13. To assemble: Put a piece of parchment or a Silpat on the counter. Invert the cake onto it and peel off the parchment or Silpat from the bottom of the cake. Use the cake ring to stamp out 2 circles from the cake. These are your top 2 cake layers. The remaining cake "scrap" will come together to make the bottom layer of the cake.

14. Clean the cake ring and place it in the center of a sheet pan lined with clean parchment or Silpat. Use 1 strip of acetate to line the inside of the cake ring. Put the cake scraps together inside the ring and use the back of your hand to stamp the scraps together into a flat, even layer.

15. Dunk a pastry brush in the birthday cake soak and give that scrap layer of cake a good, healthy bath of half of the soak. Use the back of a spoon to spread ⅓ of the frosting in an even layer over the cake. Sprinkle ⅓ of the birthday crumbs evenly over the frosting. Use the back of your hand to anchor them in place. Use the back of a spoon to spread a second fifth of the birthday cake frosting as evenly as possible over the crumbs.

16. Now for the middle layer. With your index finger, gently tuck the second strip of acetate between the cake ring and the top ¼ inch of the first strip of acetate, so that you have a clear ring of acetate 5 to 6 inches tall—high enough to support the height of the finished cake. Set a cake round on top of the frosting, and repeat the process for layer 1—cake soak, frosting, crumb, frosting. (If 1 of your 2 cake rounds is jankier than the other, use it here in the middle and save the prettier one for the top).

17. Nestle the remaining cake round into the frosting. Cover the top of the cake with the remaining frosting. Give it volume and swirls, or do as we do and opt for a perfectly flat top. Garnish the frosting with the remaining birthday crumbs.

18. Transfer the sheet pan to the freezer and freeze for a minimum of 12 hours to set the cake and filling. The cake will keep in the freezer for up to 2 weeks. At least 3 hours before you are ready to serve the cake, pull the sheet pan out of the freezer and, using your fingers and thumbs, pop the cake out of the cake ring. Gently peel off the acetate, and transfer the cake to a platter or cake stand. Let it defrost in the fridge for a minimum of 3 hours. Slice the cake into wedges and serve.

Ultimate S'mores Cake

Courtney Rich, baking blogger (*Cake by Courtney*)

Makes one three-layer, 8-inch cake or one four-layer, 6-inch cake

For the crust:

2 cups graham cracker crumbs, about 18 crackers

½ cup (1 stick) unsalted butter, melted

⅓ cup granulated sugar

For the cake:

1¾ cups plus 2 tablespoons all-purpose flour

2 cups minus 2 tablespoons granulated sugar

¾ cup dark cocoa powder

2 teaspoons baking soda

¾ teaspoon baking powder

1 teaspoon salt

1 cup buttermilk, room temperature

½ cup vegetable oil

3 large eggs, room temperature

1 teaspoon pure vanilla extract

1 cup hot water

For the marshmallow filling
(adapted from sweetapolita.com):

24 large white marshmallows

1 cup (2 sticks) unsalted butter, room temperature

1 cup powdered sugar, measured then sifted

½ teaspoon pure vanilla extract

1 jar (about 7 ounces) marshmallow fluff

This isn't a cake; this is an experience. And not just because it takes a long time to make the layers of graham cracker crust, chocolate ganache, chocolate cake, and toasted marshmallow filling. (Not to mention the chocolate buttercream frosting and marshmallow topping.) No, Courtney Rich's s'mores cake is a sugar-filled mound of spiritual enlightenment, a holy pilgrimage to the promised land of fluffy, chocolatey perfection that will shake you to your core and change you as a human being. Or maybe just make you very popular with whomever you choose to share it with.

This is what I call an intimibake. There are so many ingredients, steps, and components that you may be tempted to say that no, you are neither worthy nor capable of the s'mores cake. But I am here to tell you that YES, you are deserving, and YES, you are qualified to handle this sacred mission. The cake will challenge and test you and then, in the end, you will eat it. You totally win.

1. Preheat the oven to 375°F. Spray three 8-inch or four 6-inch round cake pans with non-stick spray and then line with parchment. Spray again and set aside.

2. In a medium bowl, combine the graham cracker crumbs, melted butter, and sugar. Stir until all the crumbs are dampened by the butter. Divide the mixture evenly among the pans and press down firmly with your hand or the back of a spoon. Bake for 5 to 7 minutes, until golden brown.

3. While the crust cools, make the cake batter. Preheat the oven to 350°F. In the bowl of an electric mixer fitted with a paddle attachment, mix the flour, sugar, cocoa, baking soda, baking powder, and salt on low speed until combined.

4. In another bowl, combine the buttermilk, oil, eggs, vanilla, and water. With the mixer on low speed, slowly add the wet ingredients to the dry, scraping the bottom of the bowl with a rubber spatula.

5. Pour the batter into the prepared pans over the graham cracker crusts (about 12 ounces in each 6-inch pan or 15 ounces in each 8-inch pan) and bake for 18 to 20 minutes, until a toothpick inserted in the center of the cake comes out clean. Cool in pans for 10 minutes, then turn them out onto a cooling rack and cool completely. Wrap in plastic wrap and chill until ready to use.

6. For the marshmallow filling, place the marshmallows on a cookie sheet lined with parchment paper and sprayed with nonstick cooking spray. Place on the middle rack of the oven and broil the marshmallows until golden brown on top, about 30 to 60 seconds. Remove the pan from the oven, gently turn the marshmallows over, and broil them again until they are golden brown on the other side. Let cool.

For the ganache:

1 cup semisweet or dark chocolate chips

½ cup heavy whipping cream

For the buttercream:

2 cups (4 sticks) unsalted butter, slightly chilled

10 ounces good quality semisweet or dark chocolate, chopped, melted, and cooled

5 cups powdered sugar, measured then sifted

pinch of salt

1 tablespoon pure vanilla extract

⅓ cup heavy whipping cream

For the marshmallow fluff:

3 egg whites, room temperature

¼ teaspoon salt

⅓ cup sugar

1 cup light Karo syrup

2 tablespoons water

1 tablespoon vanilla bean paste or clear vanilla extract

7. In the bowl of a stand mixer fitted with the paddle attachment, combine the butter and powdered sugar and beat on low until blended. Add the vanilla and mix on medium speed for about 3 minutes. With the mixer on low speed, add the marshmallow cream and cooled toasted marshmallows, and mix for about 1 minute. Set this aside until you're ready to assemble.

8. To make the ganache, pour the cream over chocolate chips in a microwave-safe bowl and heat for 45 to 60 seconds. Stir, and if needed, heat for another 30 seconds to melt the chocolate chips completely. Let cool to room temperature before using.

9. Next up is the buttercream. In the bowl of a stand mixer fitted with the paddle attachment, beat the butter until smooth and light in color, about 2 minutes. With the mixer on low speed, gradually stream in the melted chocolate. Scrape down the sides of the bowl and mix for another minute.

10. Gradually add the powdered sugar, 1 cup at a time, followed by the salt and vanilla. Add the heavy cream and then turn the mixer to medium-high speed and beat for 5 minutes.

11. The last element to make is the fluff. Whisk the egg whites and salt in the bowl of a stand mixer until fluffy and frothy. Meanwhile, heat the sugar, corn syrup, water, and vanilla paste over a medium flame until the sugar is dissolved and just simmering, about 5 minutes.

12. With the mixer on medium speed, add a tiny bit of the hot sugar mixture to the egg whites at a time. (Temper the eggs; don't scramble them.) When all the sugar is added, turn the mixer up to high and beat for 5 minutes, or until very stiff and shiny. This is best used quickly.

13. Time to assemble! Level each chocolate layer, if needed, and then place the first cake layer, graham cracker side down, on a cake board. Spread half the chocolate ganache on the cake layer and freeze 5 to 10 minutes to set the ganache a little. Carefully spread half the toasted marshmallow filling over the chocolate ganache, and repeat the ganache layer and marshmallow layer for the second cake layer, freezing between the ganache and marshmallow layers.

14. Place the final cake layer, graham cracker side down, on top, and cover with a crumb coat (thin, imperfect layer to seal in crumbs) of the chocolate frosting. Freeze the cake for 10 to 15 minutes to set the crumb coat. Finish frosting the cake with the chocolate frosting and decorate the top with the marshmallow fluff, toasting with a kitchen torch if you happen to have one.

Strawberry Champagne Cupcakes

Sophie Kallinis LaMontagne and Katherine Kallinis Berman,
cofounders of Georgetown Cupcake

Makes 24 cupcakes

For the cupcakes:

2½ cups sifted all-purpose flour

2½ teaspoons sifted baking powder

¼ teaspoon salt

½ cup (1 stick) European-style unsalted butter, room temperature

1¾ cups granulated sugar

2 large eggs, room temperature

2¼ teaspoons Madagascar Bourbon pure vanilla extract

1¼ cups whole milk, room temperature

1 teaspoon Madagascar Bourbon vanilla bean paste

¾ cup diced fresh strawberries

¾ cup champagne

For the frosting:

2 cups (4 sticks) European-style unsalted butter, room temperature

8 cups sifted confectioners' sugar

⅛ teaspoon salt

2 teaspoons whole milk, room temperature

2 teaspoons Madagascar Bourbon pure vanilla extract

½ cup champagne

strawberries, for garnish

If you ever watched the TLC show *DC Cupcakes*, filmed at sisters Sophie and Katherine's Georgetown Cupcake shop, then you know that cupcake crises are real, and that they often involve panic attacks and breakdowns. Of course once you've eaten a Georgetown cupcake, you know just how breakdown and panic attack–worthy these little clouds of cake are. They're just so freaking good.

These beautifully balanced strawberry champagne numbers are laced with fresh berries and a kiss of bubbly in both the cake and the frosting. And thanks to the sisters sharing this recipe, you, too, can have your very own, full-blown Georgetown Cupcake crisis! Or maybe just a minor emergency when you forget to set out the butter, milk, and eggs beforehand to get them to room temperature. (Consider this your warning to set out the butter, milk, and eggs!)

1. Preheat the oven to 350°F. Line two standard cupcake pans with 12 baking cups each.

2. Sift together the flour, baking powder, and salt in a bowl and set aside. Place the butter in the bowl of a stand mixer or handheld electric mixer. Beat on medium speed until fluffy. Stop to add the sugar; beat on medium speed until well incorporated. Add the eggs one at a time, mixing slowly after each addition.

3. Combine the vanilla extract and milk in a large liquid measuring cup. On low speed, add ⅓ of the flour mixture to the butter mixture, then gradually add ⅓ of the milk mixture, beating until well incorporated. Add another ⅓ of the flour mixture, followed by ⅓ of the milk mixture. Stop to scrape down the bowl as needed. Add the remaining flour mixture, followed by the remaining milk mixture, and beat just until combined.

4. Add in the vanilla bean paste and mix on low speed until just combined. Add in the diced strawberries and mix on low speed until just combined. Add in the champagne and mix on low speed until just combined.

5. Use a standard-size ice cream scoop to fill each cupcake paper with batter so that the wells are ⅔ full. Bake for 24 to 25 minutes (start checking at 23 minutes), or until a toothpick inserted into the center of a cupcake comes out clean. Transfer the pans to wire racks to cool completely.

6. For the frosting, place the unsalted butter in the bowl of a stand mixer. On low speed, add the confectioners' sugar slowly, and then beat on medium speed until well incorporated. Add the salt, milk, and vanilla extract and beat on high speed until combined.

7. Add the champagne slowly, in thirds, mixing slowly between each addition, and then whip on higher speed until light and airy, for approximately 3 to 5 minutes.

8. Transfer to a plastic piping bag fitted with a plain round metal tip. Frost each cupcake with Georgetown Cupcake's signature swirl: Hold piping bag ¼ inch above the center of the cupcake. Starting in the center of the cupcake, squeeze frosting with a burst of pressure and move piping bag in a circular motion with constant pressure, ending in the center with another burst of pressure. Top with fresh strawberries.

Red Velvet Layer Cake

Tanya Holland, owner of Brown Sugar Kitchen in Oakland, CA

Makes two 9-inch cakes

For the cake:

2½ cups all-purpose flour

1½ cups sugar

1 tablespoon natural cocoa powder

1 teaspoon baking soda

1 teaspoon kosher salt

2 eggs

1 cup buttermilk

1½ cups canola oil

2 tablespoons red food coloring

1 teaspoon distilled white vinegar

1 teaspoon vanilla extract

For the cream cheese frosting:

1 cup (2 sticks) unsalted butter, room temperature

1 pound cream cheese, room temperature

4 cups powdered sugar, sifted

1 teaspoon vanilla extract

1 cup coarsely chopped walnuts or pecans, toasted (optional)

If you haven't experienced Brown Sugar Kitchen's red velvet cake for yourself, this is the real deal. Not the gimmicky let's-make-red-velvet-flavored-potato-chips-and-scented-candles red velvet, but rich, not exactly chocolate but also not exactly vanilla, cake topped with the sweet tang of cream cheese frosting. While the red velvetization of American junk food and personal products has thankfully waned, the Southern cake staple, also thankfully, endures.

1. Preheat the oven to 350°F. Butter and flour two 9-inch round cake pans.

2. In the bowl of a stand mixer fitted with the paddle attachment, sift together the flour, sugar, cocoa, baking soda, and salt. In a medium bowl, whisk the eggs, buttermilk, oil, food coloring, vinegar, and vanilla.

3. With the mixer on low speed, slowly pour the egg mixture into the flour mixture and beat until the batter becomes smooth and ribbon-like, scraping the bowl as needed.

4. Scrape the batter into the prepared pans and smooth on top. Bake until the sides pull away from the pan and a toothpick stuck into the centers of the cakes comes out clean, 35 to 40 minutes. Let the cakes cool in the pans on a wire rack for about 10 minutes. Invert the cakes onto the rack to let completely cool before frosting. (To make ahead, cover the cakes tightly with plastic wrap, and refrigerate for up to 24 hours, or freeze for up to 2 weeks. If frozen, thaw the layers before assembling the cake.)

5. To make the frosting: Using a stand mixer fitted with the paddle attachment, combine the butter and cream cheese and mix on medium speed until combined. Reduce the speed to low, add the powdered sugar and vanilla, and beat until just combined. Continue mixing, gradually increasing the speed to medium-high, until the frosting is smooth.

6. Place 1 cake layer, bottom-side up, on a cake stand or serving plate. Using an offset spatula, spread the top of the layer with about ⅓ of the frosting. Place the second layer, bottom-side up, on top of the first layer, and spread the remaining frosting over the top and sides of the cake. Press the walnuts (if using) into the sides of the cake. Refrigerate the cake until ready to serve. The cake is best served within 1 day of being baked. To store any leftovers, press plastic wrap against the cut surfaces of the cake and top with a cake cover or a large bowl and store for up to 2 days.

Death by Chocolate Cake

Liz Marek, baking blogger (*Sugar Geek Show*)

Makes two 8-inch cakes

For the cake:

14 ounces stout beer, such as Guinness, room temperature

1½ tablespoons espresso powder

2 teaspoons vanilla

3 cups cake flour

1½ cups Dutch-processed cocoa powder

1½ teaspoons salt

1 teaspoon baking powder

2 teaspoons baking soda

1¼ cups (2½ sticks) unsalted butter, room temperature

2¼ cups sugar

4 large eggs, room temperature

¾ cup mayonnaise

6 ounces (about 1 cup) mini chocolate chips

For the chocolate buttercream:

3½ cups powdered sugar

½ cup cocoa powder, sifted

4 pasteurized egg whites (or 4 ounces)

2 cups (4 sticks) unsalted butter, room temperature

1 tablespoon vanilla extract

1 teaspoon salt

For the ganache drip:

8 ounces (about 1½ cups) semisweet chocolate

½ cup heavy whipping cream

There are two types of people in this world: those who love chocolate, and those who would sacrifice their firstborn child/pug/espresso machine for chocolate. And sure, there may be a third group who claim to not love chocolate, but they're just trying too hard to be different and aren't to be trusted. For the trustworthy chocolate lovers, there must be chocolate cake with chocolate frosting, and what makes Liz Marek's cake so special is that it's topped with both chocolate buttercream *and* chocolate ganache. That's the kind of chocolate-on-chocolate action that makes a person forsake a pug.

1. Preheat the oven to 335°F. Prepare cake pans (this recipe makes two 8-inch cakes) with nonstick spray and/or parchment paper.

2. In a large measuring cup, combine the beer, espresso powder, and vanilla. Whisk together and set aside. In a large bowl, sift together the flour, cocoa powder, salt, baking powder, and baking soda and set aside.

3. Place the softened butter in the bowl of a stand mixer with the paddle attachment. Cream until smooth and shiny. With the mixer on low, gradually sprinkle in the sugar. Mix on medium-high until mixture is fluffy and almost white, about 3 to 5 minutes.

4. Reduce the speed back to low. Add eggs one at a time. Let the egg incorporate fully before adding in the next egg to avoid breaking your batter. Add in your mayo and mix until combined.

5. With the mixer on low, add in ⅓ of your dry ingredients and mix until almost combined. Add in ⅓ of your liquid ingredients. Repeat the process 2 more times until everything

is combined. Fold in mini chocolate chips.

6. Divide the cake batter into your cake pans and bake for 40 to 45 minutes, until a toothpick comes out cleanly but with a few sticky crumbs. Don't overbake. Let your cakes cool in the pan for 10 to 15 minutes before turning out onto a cooling rack. Let fully cool, then gently wrap in plastic wrap and chill until the cakes are firm enough to handle. You can flash chill in the freezer if you need to cool them quickly.

7. For the chocolate buttercream, sift together the powdered sugar and cocoa powder. Place pasteurized egg whites, powdered sugar, and cocoa powder in the bowl of your stand mixer. Attach the whisk, combine ingredients on low, and then whip on high for 5 minutes.

8. Add in your softened butter in chunks. Add in vanilla and salt. Whisk on high until light and fluffy. (Optional: Switch to a paddle attachment and mix on low for 15 to 20 minutes to make the buttercream very smooth and remove air bubbles.) Frost that cake!

9. For the ganache drip, microwave chocolate for 30 seconds to get it warm. Heat cream on the stove over medium heat just until it starts to simmer. Do not boil. Pour over chocolate and let sit for 5 minutes. Whisk until smooth. If you have lumps, place the bowl into a microwave for 30 seconds and whisk. Let the ganache cool until it's barely warm to the touch. Place the ganache into a piping bag and drizzle over the top of your frosted and chilled cake.

Lemon Layer Cake with Lemon Curd and Sugared Blueberries

Sugar Bakeshop in Charleston, SC

Makes two 9-inch cakes

For the vanilla cake:

1½ cups (3 sticks) butter, room temperature

3 cups granulated white sugar

6 large eggs, room temperature

3 teaspoons vanilla extract

4½ cups all-purpose flour

1½ teaspoons table salt (not kosher)

1½ tablespoons baking powder

1½ cups whole milk

For the lemon curd:

1 cup granulated white sugar

3 large eggs

zest of 2 lemons

1 cup fresh lemon juice, strained

½ cup (1 stick) butter, melted

For the lemon buttercream frosting:

3 cups (6 sticks) butter

zest from 2 lemons

up to 14 cups powdered sugar, sifted (depending on desired level of sweetness)

½ cup heavy cream

¼ teaspoon yellow food dye, optional (added to heavy cream)

6 tablespoons fresh lemon juice, strained

I have done lemons wrong, and I am so, so sorry. It's my loss—lemons have gone about their bright, zippy existence blissfully unaware of my aversion to them—and I truly grieve those three-plus decades of missing out on splendidly tangy desserts. But I am reformed, and now a proud card-carrying member of the lemon-desserts-are-the-best-desserts club. Sugar Bakeshop's vanilla cake with lemon curd filling and lemon frosting is exactly why, and I believe it can turn even the most lemon-reluctant. It's the ideal marriage of sweet and sour, and you will want to scoop up every last drop of the lemon curd with your fingers, like I do. Just making up for lost time.

1. Preheat the oven to 350°F (325°F if using convection). In a stand mixer, cream butter and sugar on low speed for 1 minute. Scrape bowl down with rubber spatula and continue to cream on medium speed for 2 minutes. Scrape down the bowl again.

2. Crack eggs into a separate bowl and add vanilla to the eggs. Add half of the eggs to the butter/sugar mixture, and on low speed, mix the eggs into the mixture for about 15 to 20 seconds. Scrape the bowl down and add the remaining eggs to mixture. Mix just until the eggs are broken up and almost mixed in, but not fully, about 15 to 20 seconds. Scrape the bowl.

3. Sift together the flour, salt, and baking powder into a separate bowl. Add ⅓ of this dry mix to the stand mixer, and on low speed, mix until the flour is almost all the way incorporated. With mixer still running, stream in ⅓ of the milk. When it's almost incorporated, stop mixer and scrape down bowl with spatula. Add the second ⅓ of the dry mix, and mix on low speed until almost incorporated. With mixer running, add the second ⅓ of the milk, and mix until almost incorporated. Stop mixer and scrape bowl down with spatula. Add the remaining dry mix to stand mixer, and mix on low speed until almost incorporated. Stream in remaining milk while mixer is running, and stop it just before it's fully incorporated. It's important not to overmix the batter. Remove bowl from stand mixer, and with rubber spatula, scrape the sides and bottom of the bowl in a folding motion. Batter should look pretty uniform at this point.

4. Trace the bottoms of your two pans onto parchment paper and cut out the circles. Spray both pans with PAM, place the parchment circle in each pan, and spray again. Be sure to coat the sides of the pan as well. Evenly divide the batter between the two pans, and smooth out the top. Place pans in center of oven, and bake for 20

For topping and assembly:

2 cups milk, for milk bath

2 cups blueberries

2 cups granulated white sugar, in a shallow bowl

minutes, then rotate the pans and bake 15 minutes. Insert a paring or butter knife into the center of the cake and pull it straight out—when it comes out (relatively) clean, the cake is done. If it isn't done, keep baking and checking on it every 5 minutes. Let the cakes cool for 5 minutes before removing from pans. Immediately wrap in plastic wrap and set aside.

5. For the lemon curd: in a microwave-safe bowl, combine sugar, eggs, and lemon zest with a whisk. Whisk in lemon juice, and then the melted butter. Cook in microwave for 2 minutes, then whisk. Cook 2 more minutes, and whisk it. Cook 1 minute, whisk, and cook 1 more minute, and whisk (total of 6 minutes). The curd should be bubbling when you whisk it—this means it's done. Place in fridge to cool—you'll want this to be completely cooled before you use it in your cake.

6. For the lemon buttercream: Cream butter and lemon zest in a stand mixer for 1 minute on low speed. Scrape down with a rubber spatula. Turn mixer up to medium speed and cream butter until light and fluffy, about 1 to 2 more minutes. With mixer off, add ⅓ of the powdered sugar to bowl and turn mixer to low speed. Mix until sugar is incorporated, then stream in the cream/food dye with the mixer still running. Mix until fully incorporated. Scrape down bowl. Add another ⅓ of the powdered sugar to the mixer and mix on low speed until combined. Slowly stream in lemon juice while the mixer is running, and mix until combined. Scrape down bowl. Add final ⅓ of powdered sugar, and mix

until fully combined. Scrape down bowl, and mix again. Don't be afraid of overmixing this, you really want to make sure the icing is totally mixed.

7. For the assembly: Unwrap cakes and place on a level surface. Use a large serrated knife to cut the domes off—this will be the top ¼" to ½", depending on how your cake baked. Still using the serrated knife, find the middle of the cake and cut in half lengthwise. Do this to both cakes. You should now have four layers of cake; two bottoms and two tops.

8. Grab your milk bath and a pastry brush, and brush the milk over the top of each cake layer. You may not use all the milk—you just want to make sure it's evenly coated. This will help keep the cake moist. Grab your (cold) lemon curd, and spoon it on the top of the two bottom layers of cake. Try to keep it from reaching the outer ½ inch of the cake, so it doesn't seep out the sides. Place the top layers of cakes on the two bottom layers.

9. Grab your buttercream for a crumb coat. Using a metal icing spatula, coat the outside of the cake in a thin layer of icing. Do this to both cakes and pop in the freezer for 20 to 30 minutes. When they're firm, put whichever cake is less even on top onto the cake stand and put a thin layer of icing on top, to act as "glue." Using your icing spatula, gently lift the second cake and place it on top of the first. Make sure the top cake is evenly centered. Using your icing spatula, ice the sides of the cakes where they meet in the middle, then pop the whole thing back in the freezer for about 10 minutes.

10. When it's nice and firm, place the cake back on the cake stand and put on the final coat of frosting. Once it's looking good, rinse the blueberries in a strainer under cold water. Shake to remove excess water. Scoop half of them into the bowl of sugar and shake around until the blueberries are evenly coated. Begin placing them on the cake—place one right in the center of the top of the cake, and then work out from there. Try to get them as close together as you can, so the entire top is covered. Once you've finished with the first cup of blueberries, repeat the drying/sugaring of the second half and continue until the top of the cake is covered.

Yum Yum Banana Coffee Cake with Cheesecake Filling and Chocolate Streusel

Mindy Segal, owner of Mindy's Bakery in Chicago, IL

Makes one 10-inch cake

For the streusel:

1½ cups all-purpose flour

½ cup packed light brown sugar

2 teaspoons kosher salt

½ cup (1 stick) unsalted butter

4 ounces dark chocolate, coarsely chopped

For the cheesecake custard filling:

6 ounces cream cheese, room temperature

¾ cup granulated sugar

1 egg

¼ cup sour cream

2 tablespoons heavy cream

1 teaspoon vanilla extract

pinch of salt

For the coffee cake:

1 cup (2 sticks) unsalted butter, room temperature

1 cup granulated sugar

2 eggs

1 teaspoon vanilla extract

2 cups all-purpose flour

2 teaspoons kosher salt

1 teaspoon baking powder

1 teaspoon baking soda

Mindy Segal is my cookie guru, and her cookbook, *Cookie Love*, is my cookie Bible. This is the first reason I was skeptical of her Yum Yum Coffee Cake recipe. Sure, I trust her completely when it comes to small, flat sweets, but could she really also be an expert when it comes to bigger, fluffier ones?

The second reason I was hesitant to give this recipe a try is because coffee cake is the only thing my mom makes really well. Like me, she's not much of a cook, but her sour cream coffee cake (which won the 1969 small fry bake-off in Glendora, California) is out of this world. Could Mindy really compete with the 1969 small fry baking champion?

As it turns out, yes.

Mindy's version has the delicious streusel and globs of sour cream mixed in like my mom's cake, but she also puts dark chocolate into her streusel, bananas into the cake batter, *and* a cheesecake custard filling. It's not really a fair competition.

It took a leap of non-cookie faith, but I've learned to trust in Mindy and to do as she tells me. Kind of like mom.

---

1. Make the streusel: Combine all dry ingredients, excluding the chocolate, in a bowl. Set aside. Cook the butter in a pot until it's brown and nutty. Remove from heat and set aside to cool, about 10 minutes. Combine the brown butter with the dry ingredients, rubbing the ingredients between your hands to form a streusel. Place in the refrigerator to cool. Once the streusel is cool, mix in the chocolate.

2. Make the cheesecake custard: Preheat the oven to 300°F. In the bowl of a stand mixer fitted with a paddle attachment, mix the cream cheese and sugar, scraping down the bottom of the bowl to combine thoroughly. Beat until smooth. Add the egg, sour cream, heavy cream, vanilla, and salt. Mix to combine. (Optional step: Strain the custard through a fine mesh strainer.)

3. Place the custard in a small casserole dish. Place the filled dish in a larger casserole dish. Fill the larger dish with 1 inch of water. Carefully transfer the dishes to the oven and bake until set, 30 to 40 minutes. Remove from the oven and let cool completely.

4. Make the cake: In a stand mixer fitted with a paddle attachment, cream the butter and sugar until light and fluffy. Scrape down bowl to make sure everything is mixed together. Add the

½ cup sour cream,
room temperature

2 ripe bananas, mashed
or puréed until smooth

eggs, one at a time, and the vanilla. Scrape down the bowl again.

5. In a separate bowl, combine the dry ingredients to the butter mixture. On low speed, add half of the dry ingredients to the butter mixture, then add the sour cream, then add the remaining dry ingredients. Add the puréed bananas. Scrape down the bowl completely so that the batter is thoroughly combined.

6. Spray a 10-inch Bundt pan with vegetable oil. Evenly sprinkle half of the streusel on the bottom of the pan. Pour half of the batter in the pan. Evenly spoon the cheesecake mixture on top of the batter. Sprinkle again with remaining streusel. Top with the rest of batter. Transfer to the oven and bake for 45 to 50 minutes. Let cool completely, unmold, and serve.

Daydream Believer Cupcakes

Kat Gordon, owner of Muddy's Bake Shop in Memphis, TN

Makes 12 to 15 cupcakes

For the cupcakes:

½ cup sour cream

2 tablespoons neutral oil, such as canola

½ teaspoon pure vanilla extract

½ teaspoon pure almond extract

1 cup buttermilk

2 cups cake flour

½ teaspoon baking soda

½ teaspoon kosher salt

1½ cups granulated sugar

½ cup (1 stick) unsalted butter, room temperature

2 large eggs, room temperature

For the buttercream:

1 cup (2 sticks) butter, softened

pinch of kosher salt

1 teaspoon vanilla extract

¼ cup apricot preserves

¼ cup heavy cream

4 to 6 cups confectioners' sugar

These almond cupcakes, gussied up with a gentle cloud of apricot buttercream, inspired a bit of a cult following at Kat Gordon's Muddy's Bake Shop, and with good reason. Like sweet with salty, sweet with a little tang (here via the sour cream) just works. Because she's no fool, Kat recommends using butter with at least 80.9 percent butterfat, as well as full-fat sour cream and buttermilk for this recipe. You're no fool, either, so go with the fat. All of the fat.

1. Preheat the oven to 350°F. Line muffin tins with cupcake papers.

2. In a medium bowl, whisk together sour cream, oil, vanilla, and almond extract. Slowly add buttermilk while whisking.

3. In the bowl of a stand mixer, whisk together the cake flour, baking soda, salt, and sugar. Slice the butter and add it to the flour mixture. Mix on low speed for 3 minutes. Keep the mixer on low speed as you add the buttermilk mixture. Pause occasionally to scrape down sides of the bowl with a rubber spatula. Add the eggs one at a time, beating between each addition. Batter should be smooth.

4. Scoop into muffin tin and bake until tops are springy to the touch and a toothpick inserted in center comes out clean, approximately 20 to 25 minutes. Cool completely before icing.

5. While cupcakes are baking and cooling, make the buttercream. Using the mixer, beat the butter and salt together until light, fluffy, and considerably paler, approximately 3 to 5 minutes on medium speed. Add the vanilla and apricot preserves and beat for 2 more minutes.

6. Add cream and sugar in parts, beating thoroughly between additions, until icing is fluffy, holds its shape on a spoon, and no longer looks shiny. (You may not need all of the cream.) Frost those cupcakes! If desired, warm some apricot preserves and drizzle over the tops.

Pound Cake

Stephanie Hart, founder of Brown Sugar Bakery, Chicago, IL

Makes one cake

1½ cups (3 sticks) salted butter, room temperature

3 cups sugar

6 eggs, room temperature

3 cups all-purpose flour

1 teaspoon baking powder

1 cup sour cream, divided

3 tablespoons vanilla

1 tablespoon lemon juice

Stephanie Hart sells a lot of crackly-bottomed pound cakes out of her Chicago bakery, and after one bite, you'll know why. "This is real pound cake, the heart recipe for me," she says. Stephanie makes the cakes as her grandma used to do, in old Jell-O molds, but you can use a Bundt or tube pan. In fact, the recipe is a version of her grandma's, only she ups the vanilla and switched from cream cheese to sour cream. (You can replace equal amounts of cream cheese, but if you do so, it's best to wait until the second day to eat the cake, and who can wait?) This cake is dangerously good by itself, but you can also jazz it up with powdered sugar, berries, caramel, fresh flowers, Skittles, LEGO people, or whatever floats your pound cake boat.

1. Preheat the oven to 325°F. Grease a 10-cup Bundt pan or 10-inch tube pan with shortening and dust with flour, or generously spray with nonstick cooking spray.

2. In the bowl of a stand mixer, cream butter and sugar together until fluffy. Scrape down the bowl and add eggs one at a time. Let the egg disappear into the batter before adding the next egg.

3. In a separate bowl, sift together the flour and baking powder. Add half of the dry mixture to butter/sugar/egg mixture and mix until just incorporated.

4. Add half of the sour cream and mix. Scrape down bowl and mix in the other half of the dry ingredients. Mix until just incorporated and then add the rest of the sour cream and mix. Scrape down the bowl and add vanilla. Mix, and add lemon juice. Scrape down the bowl and mix everything until combined.

5. Spoon the batter into your prepared pan. Bake 75 to 85 minutes. Start checking at 75 minutes—the cake is done when a toothpick comes out clean or with dry crumbs. Cool for 10 minutes before inverting the cake onto a wire rack or plate to release.

Chocolate Pound Cake with Caramel Icing

Jocelyn Delk Adams, baking blogger (*Grandbaby Cakes*)

Makes one cake

For the pound cake:

¼ cup semisweet chocolate chips

1½ cups (3 sticks) unsalted butter, room temperature

2¾ cups granulated sugar

5 large eggs, room temperature

2¼ cups sifted all-purpose flour

¾ cup unsweetened cocoa powder

½ teaspoon instant coffee powder

½ teaspoon baking powder

½ teaspoon salt

1⅓ cups buttermilk, room temperature

1 tablespoon pure vanilla extract

For the caramel icing:

6 tablespoons unsalted butter

1 12-ounce can evaporated milk

1 cup granulated sugar

1 teaspoon pure vanilla extract

pinch of salt

I never knew the difference between frosting and icing. When cake expert Jocelyn Delk Adams mentioned her caramel icing, I assumed she was using the word as a synonym for frosting, something I've probably done my whole life. (This is why she's the cake expert, and I am not.) But the two words aren't interchangeable. Frosting is thicker and fluffier, which is why it's typically used to cover cakes. Icing, meanwhile, is thinner and glossier, and it's used as more of a glaze, like as the caramelicious, drippy topping for her chocolate pound cake.

Jocelyn's caramel icing recipe comes from her Aunt Bev, who, she says, "definitely gets down in the kitchen." You, too, will need to be prepared to get down, because the icing takes an hour of standing at the stove, stirring constantly. There are no shortcuts to heaven, kids, and it takes that long to develop its rich, luscious flavor. But when you get there, you will understand that good things come to those who wait, and by "understand," I mean you will be licking the caramel off the spoon and probably off your fingers and also out of the pot, and hopefully you'll save enough for the cake because you don't want to stand at the stove stirring for another hour. But you would, because it's so worth it.

1. Preheat the oven to 325°F. Liberally grease a 12-cup Bundt pan with the nonstick method of your choice.

2. Pour the chocolate chips into a medium microwave-safe bowl. Microwave on high for 15 seconds at a time, stirring after each heating interval, until the chocolate is completely melted. Allow the chocolate to cool down.

3. In the bowl of your stand mixer fitted with the paddle or whisk attachment, beat the butter for 2 minutes on high speed. Slowly add the granulated sugar. Cream together for an additional 5 minutes, until very pale yellow and fluffy. Add the eggs one at a time, combining well after each addition and scraping down the sides and bottom of the bowl as needed.

4. Turn your mixer down to its lowest speed and slowly add the flour in 2 batches until just combined. Be careful not to overbeat. Add the cocoa powder, coffee powder, baking powder, and salt. Lastly, add the melted chocolate, buttermilk, and vanilla extract. Make sure the chocolate has cooled somewhat before adding so as to not curdle the buttermilk. Scrape down the sides and bottom of the bowl and mix the batter until just combined. Be careful to not overmix.

5. Pour the batter into the prepared pan and bake for 70 to 80 minutes, or until a toothpick inserted into the center of the cake comes out clean. Check frequently to ensure you do not overbake this cake.

6. Let the cake cool in the pan on a wire rack for 10 minutes, then invert onto a serving plate. Let cool to room temperature. Lightly cover the cake with foil or plastic wrap so it does not dry out.

7. For the caramel icing, add butter, evaporated milk, and sugar to a saucepan over medium-low heat until everything has melted together.

8. Leave over medium to low heat, stirring consistently, for about 45 minutes to 1 hour. Watch the entire time to make sure it does not burn until thickened and caramel has darkened to a beautiful golden brown. It should also thickly coat the back of a spoon to ensure thickness.

9. Remove from heat and add in vanilla extract and salt. Cool for about 15 to 20 minutes to allow it to thicken somewhat before icing the cake. Carefully pour over the top of the completely room-temperature cake, let set, then serve.

Carrot Cake with Cream Cheese Frosting

Astrid Field, baking blogger (*The Sweet Rebellion*)

Makes one three-layer, 8-inch cake

For the cake:

2 cups soft brown sugar

1½ cups sunflower oil

4 large eggs

1 teaspoon vanilla

3¼ cups all-purpose flour

1½ teaspoons baking soda

1½ teaspoons baking powder

½ teaspoon salt

1 teaspoon ground cinnamon

2 teaspoons mixed spice
(see below, or substitute
with pumpkin pie spice)

3½ cups carrots, grated

1 cup walnuts, roughly chopped

For the frosting:

¾ cup (1½ sticks) unsalted
butter, softened

11 ounces (1⅓ packages)
cream cheese, softened

6 cups powdered sugar

2 teaspoons vanilla

For the mixed spice:

1 tablespoon cinnamon

1 teaspoon ground allspice

1 teaspoon ground ginger

½ teaspoon ground cloves

½ teaspoon nutmeg

½ teaspoon coriander seed

You could be one of those people who waits until Easter to make this melt-in-your-mouth, just-spicy-enough carrot cake, depriving yourself of its deliciousness 364 days a year. Or, you could commit the ultimate act of bravery, defying expectations and making this cake in September. And June. And maybe January and August, too. Bake it whenever you crave vitamin A and cinnamon, you carrot cake maverick, you.

Astrid Field's recipe calls for mixed spice, as prevalent on shelves in her native South Africa as pumpkin pie spice is here. It's almost the same thing, they're just not as PSL crazed as we are.

1. Preheat the oven to 335°F. Grease and line three 8-inch cake pans with parchment paper.

2. Place brown sugar, oil, eggs, and vanilla into a large bowl and beat well. Gradually add the flour, baking soda, baking powder, salt, and spices. Beat until well combined. Stir in grated carrots and chopped walnuts.

3. Divide the mixture equally among the 3 prepared cake pans. Bake 35 to 40 minutes, or until a toothpick inserted into the centers comes out clean. Leave the cakes to cool in the pans for 5 minutes, then turn them out onto cooling racks to cool completely.

4. For the frosting, beat the softened butter and cream cheese together until smooth. Sift in the powdered sugar 1 cup at a time, beating well after each addition. Mix in the vanilla.

5. Once the cakes have cooled, place one of them onto a serving plate and spread on ¼ of the frosting. Place the second cake on top and spread on another ¼ of the frosting. Top with the last cake. Roughly frost the top and outside of the cake with a crumb coat (a thin layer of frosting that seals in stray crumbs). Refrigerate for 45 minutes, then use the remaining frosting to cover the cake completely. Smooth neatly, then decorate with fresh flowers or chopped walnuts.

Olive Oil Cake

Angela Renee Chase, co-owner of Flora Bodega & Paseo
Farmers Market in Oklahoma City, OK

Makes one 8-inch cake

2 cups organic flour

⅔ cup organic sugar

1 teaspoon baking soda

1 teaspoon baking powder

1 teaspoon fine sea salt

⅔ cup olive oil

**zest of citrus fruit, like
an orange or lemon**

**⅓ cup juice (any citrus or 2
tablespoons apple cider vinegar)**

⅔ cup Greek yogurt

2 large eggs

I remember the first time I saw olive oil cake on a menu. I was so confused. Olive oil had only a savory connotation in my young mind, and I didn't grasp that its moisture-inducing properties put butter to shame. One bite of the bright, dewy cake swayed me to the EVOO side, and this zippy, citrusy version by Angela Chase will do the same for anyone.

1. Preheat the oven to 365°F. Use olive oil to grease an 8-inch round cake pan and dust with flour. Trace the pan on parchment paper, cut out the circle, and lay on bottom of greased pan.

2. Combine dry ingredients in a mixing bowl. In a separate bowl, pour in oil and then zest in citrus. Add juice (or apple cider vinegar) and yogurt and whisk until combined.

3. In a small bowl, whisk eggs with a fork. Combine with wet mixture and whisk again. Pour into the bowl with dry ingredients and fold/stir with a spatula until nearly all mixed.

4. Pour into the cake pan and smooth out any surface lumps with a spatula or spoon. Place on the bottom rack of oven and bake for 15 to 20 minutes. Rotate the pan and bake for another 5 to 10 minutes. Move the pan to the top rack and finish baking for 15 to 20 minutes. Remove from oven and let rest once finished. When fully cooled, tap sides of pan on table or counter to pop out the cake.

CHAPTER 3

Pies & Tarts

STRAWBERRY HAND PIES   76
Tracy Wilk, from #BakeItForward

CLASSIC APPLE PIE   79
The Upper Crust Pie Bakery in Overland Park, KS

**PASSION FRUIT PIE WITH
MACADAMIA LACE BRITTLE   80**
Darcy Schein and Leslie Coale-Mossman,
owners of Pie Junkie in Oklahoma City, OK

**BLUEBERRY LEMON PIE
(THE BOY SCOUT)   83**
Shauna Lott Harman, owner/chief pie maker
at The Long I Pie Shop in Denver, CO

**STRAWBERRY LABNEH
GRANOLA TART   84**
Majed Ali, baking blogger (The Cinnaman)

CHOCOLATE CARAMEL TART   88
Erica Leahy, Three Daughters
Baking in Maplewood, NJ

PEANUT BUTTER PIE   91
Kelli Marks, Sweet Love Bakes in Little Rock, AR

BLUEBERRY GALETTE   92
Jennifer Essex, owner of Ruby Jean
Patisserie in Denver, CO

Strawberry Hand Pies

Tracy Wilk, from *#BakeItForward*

Makes six hand pies

For the crust:

1¾ cups all-purpose flour

1½ teaspoons granulated sugar

1 teaspoon kosher salt

½ cup (1 stick) + 2 tablespoons cold, unsalted butter, cubed

½ cup ice-cold water

For the filling:

2 cups strawberries, trimmed

2 tablespoons granulated sugar

2 teaspoons cornstarch

zest and juice of 1 lime

For assembly:

1 egg mixed with 1 teaspoon water, for egg wash

granulated sugar, to sprinkle on top

I tend to think of myself as a pie hater. I'm a card-carrying member of #teamcake or #teamchocolate or #teamanythingbutpie. The more accurate story is that I'm a bad pie hater, and there are just so many bad pies out there. These strawberry hand pies—and the other flaky-crusted masterpieces in this book—have taught me that I've been too hard on pie. As the rest of humanity knows, pie is freaking amazing, and—dare I say it—maybe even more deliciously nuanced than cake. Even better, these cute little pies were a part of Tracy Wilk's #BakeItForward movement during the pandemic, where she delivered fresh-baked treats to frontline workers in New York City. Good pie + good deeds = #teampie.

1. Whisk the flour, sugar, and salt together in a large mixing bowl. Rub the butter into the dry ingredients by hand and mix until the butter is reduced to small pieces about the size of a pea.

2. Slowly add about half of the water. Using a rubber spatula (or your hands), bring the dough together. Add water as needed to achieve the right consistency. There will be lumps of butter remaining in the dough, and the dough should hold its shape when squeezed. If it is too sticky, add a small amount of flour. If it is too dry, add a small amount of water.

3. Wrap the pie dough tightly in plastic wrap and refrigerate until firm, 1 to 2 hours. The dough can also rest in the refrigerator overnight.

4. For the filling: Combine all the ingredients in a small pot and cook over medium heat until the strawberries begin to break down and the mixture begins to thicken, about 8

minutes. Place in a bowl and set aside to fully cool. Line a cookie tray with parchment paper and set aside.

5. Preheat the oven to 375°F. Lightly flour a work surface, and, using a rolling pin, roll the pie dough until it is about ⅛-inch thick. Using a 4-inch round cutter, cut out rounds and place them on a prepared cookie tray.

6. Using a pastry brush, create a border of egg wash on half of the rounds. Spoon strawberry filling into the center and top with the second half of the rounds. Pinch the outside, releasing any air bubbles. Using a fork, crimp the edges. Using a paring knife, cut an X in the center of each pie.

7. Brush the top of the hand pies with egg wash and sprinkle with sugar. Bake for about 20 to 30 minutes, until golden brown and the fruit is bubbling. Allow to cool for at least 5 minutes before removing from the sheet tray.

Classic Apple Pie

The Upper Crust Pie Bakery in Overland Park, KS

Makes one pie

For the double crust:

2 cups (4 sticks) unsalted butter, chilled and cut into small chunks

5 cups flour, plus extra for rolling

1 teaspoon salt

1 teaspoon sugar

ice water, approximately ¾ cup

For the filling:

4 to 5 cups peeled, sliced apples (The Upper Crust uses Fuji or Jonagold, but their grandmother's first choice was Jonathan apples)

1 cup granulated sugar

¼ cup all-purpose flour

¼ teaspoon nutmeg

¼ teaspoon salt

1 tablespoon lemon juice

1 tablespoon butter, cubed

1 beaten egg, to brush on top crust

sugar for sprinkling on top crust

An apple pie recipe should come from somebody's grandmother, preferably a grandmother from the Midwest. This one comes from Jan Knobel and Elaine Van Buskirk's grandmother, and it's the exact apple pie the girls grew up eating in central Kansas. This pie does not require any MoMA-worthy top crust designs or styling apple slices into a perfect rose.

It probably won't get the most likes on your Instagram page, and it may not qualify as food porn. Now I never met Jan and Elaine's grandmother, but I'm guessing she'd be fine with her apple pie not being considered food porn. It's an excellent apple pie, and that's more than enough.

1. In a large bowl, work the butter into the flour, salt, and sugar with your hands until you have pea-sized lumps of butter. Pour in small amounts of ice water at a time, gently incorporating just enough to moisten the dough. When the dough holds together on its own, stop mixing. Divide the dough into 3 or 4 balls and form each into a disk shape. Chill the dough before rolling it out.

2. For the filling, measure apples into a large mixing bowl. In a smaller bowl, mix the sugar, flour, nutmeg, and salt. Pour that over the sliced apples and gently toss.

3. Preheat the oven to 375°F. Transfer the apple mixture to an unbaked pie shell rolled out and placed in pie plate, pressing apples down gently to remove extra space between slices. Drizzle with lemon juice and top with cubed butter pieces.

4. Cover with top crust. Trim edges with scissors, leaving about 1 to 2 inches of overhang. Roll the top and bottom edges together underhand so that they're sealed and sit on the rim of the pie plate. Crimp the edge, then brush with a beaten egg. Vent top crust, allowing steam to escape during baking. Sprinkle top with sugar— Upper Crust uses both granulated and turbinado.

5. Bake until golden brown and thickened filling is bubbling from center, approximately 1 hour.

Passion Fruit Pie with Macadamia Lace Brittle

Darcy Schein and Leslie Coale-Mossman, owners of Pie Junkie in Oklahoma City, OK

Makes one 9-inch pie

For the pie:

1 8.8-ounce package Biscoff cookies

½ cup (1 stick) unsalted butter, melted

2 14-ounce cans sweetened condensed milk

⅔ cup passion fruit puree or pulp

6 egg yolks

2 cups heavy cream

½ cup powdered sugar

For the brittle:

¾ cup light brown sugar

½ cup (1 stick) butter

½ cup light corn syrup

½ teaspoon vanilla

½ teaspoon salt

¾ cup flour

¾ cup macadamia nuts, finely chopped

If you, like me, are intimidated by pie making, this is the perfect starter pie. For one, the hardest part is finding passion fruit puree (check Amazon, Mexican grocers, or even Walmart), and for another, you get the added bonus of getting to lick prebaked buttery brittle off your fingers.

The crust doesn't involve any crimping or cutting cold butter or any of that doughy nonsense—just throw your cookies in a food processor, hit a button, and watch it whirl itself together. The filling is even easier—just three ingredients!—and if that's not enough to ease your pie anxiety, there's versatility in this recipe, too. While the passion fruit custard is pretty killer, Darcy and Leslie say you could try other purees, like mango, or sub pecans, walnuts, or cashews in the brittle.

1. Preheat the oven to 350°F. Crush cookies in food processor and pour into mixing bowl. Mix in the melted butter and stir until cookie crumbs are fairly wet and hold together when balled into the palm of your hand. Press cookie crumbs into a sprayed 9-inch pie plate and pack tightly, all the way up the sides. Set in refrigerator while making filling.

2. For the filling: Combine sweetened condensed milk, passion fruit puree, and egg yolks by hand in a mixing bowl. Make sure it's well mixed and no ribbons of sweetened condensed milk are visible. Pour filling into crust and smooth the top of the pie with a rubber spatula, breaking any bubbles. Place pie in oven and bake for 15 to 18 minutes (12 to 15 on convection), rotating midway. The pie is ready when the edges start to bubble. Set aside to cool for about an hour and then transfer to refrigerator. Let it cool for at least 4 hours.

3. To make the brittle, combine brown sugar, butter, corn syrup, vanilla, and salt in a small pot and cook on medium heat until sugar has dissolved. Remove from heat and stir in flour and nuts. Let sit for 5 to 10 minutes.

4. Line a cookie sheet with parchment paper or silicone baking mat. Scoop brittle batter using a teaspoon or small scoop onto the sheet. Leave 3 to 4 inches between each scoop, as the batter will spread. Bake at 350°F for 8 to 10 minutes, or until brittle is spread and very brown. It should look lacy and see-through. Let cool 10 minutes before transferring to an airtight container.

5. When ready to serve your pie, combine cream and powdered sugar with a hand mixer or stand mixer fitted with whisk attachment and mix on

high until firm. If you have extra puree and want to amp up your whipped cream, add a dash to the bowl. You can pipe your whipped cream in a fun border around the pie or, if that stresses you out, just plop a dollop onto each slice. Top with brittle webs or chards and you're good to go!

Blueberry Lemon Pie (The Boy Scout)

Shauna Lott Harman, owner/chief pie maker at The Long I Pie Shop in Denver, CO

Makes one 9-inch pie

For the crust:

2½ cups all-purpose flour

1 tablespoon granulated sugar

1 teaspoon salt

1 cup (2 sticks) unsalted butter, cold

¾ cup cold water

For the lemon custard:

6 eggs, lightly beaten

1 cup granulated sugar

½ cup (1 stick) unsalted butter, cubed

⅓ cup lemon juice

2 teaspoons lemon zest

For the blueberry compote:

3 cups blueberries

⅓ cup granulated sugar

1 tablespoon cornstarch

¼ cup orange juice

The secret to Shauna Lott Harman's marvelously flaky, extra-crispy crusts? She bakes her pies in a cast iron skillet, a genius move that results in a perfectly even cook on the crust. For her blueberry lemon version, which she's nicknamed The Boy Scout, she layers sweet blueberry compote over a tart lemon custard. You should probably have one in your oven right now, because, you know, Be Prepared.

1. Mix dry ingredients in a large bowl. Cube the unsalted butter and add it to the flour mixture. Cut butter into flour mixture using a pastry blender until cold butter is marble sized.

2. Gradually pour in water, mixing with hands until you can form a ball and the dough feels like Play-Doh. Tightly wrap with cling wrap and refrigerate for at least 2 hours before using.

3. In a medium saucepan, combine lightly beaten eggs, 1 cup granulated sugar, cubed butter, lemon juice, and lemon zest. While constantly stirring mixture over medium heat, cook for 20 minutes, or until thick. Remove from heat and let lemon custard cool for at least 15 minutes.

4. In a small saucepan, toss blueberries and ⅓ cup granulated sugar. In a small bowl, combine orange juice and cornstarch until smooth. Mix orange juice and cornstarch mixture with the blueberries in the saucepan. Cook over medium heat until mixture comes to a boil (approximately 3 minutes), while stirring gently. Cook another 2 minutes as it bubbles. Remove blueberries from heat and let them cool at least 15 minutes.

5. Preheat the oven to 400°F. Divide pie crust in two; half goes into the bottom of a 9-inch cast iron skillet and half is for the top crust lattice. Pour lemon custard into the unbaked bottom pie crust, then pour blueberry mixture on top. Lattice the top of the pie with 1-inch-wide strips of crust. Roll or crimp your edges. Bake in skillet for 50 to 60 minutes. Let cool on counter at least 2 hours before eating.

Strawberry Labneh Granola Tart

Majed Ali, baking blogger (*The Cinnaman*)

Makes one 9-inch tart

For the crust:

3 cups granola, without any dried fruit

¼ teaspoon sea salt

1 tablespoon granulated sugar

1 teaspoon cinnamon

⅓ cup (just over 5 tablespoons) butter, melted

For the filling:

3 large eggs

zest of 2 limes

¼ cup confectioners' sugar, sifted

½ teaspoon sea salt

1 teaspoon good quality vanilla paste

2 cups labneh

For honey lime syrup and topping:

¼ cup honey

¼ cup lime juice

1¼ cups fresh strawberries, hulled and sliced

The main ingredients in this tart are labneh (an extra-strained, thick, tangy yogurt popular in the Middle East), granola, and strawberries. It's definitely healthy-ish, and you could probably get away with eating it for breakfast. (OK, let's be real. I've probably eaten everything in this book for breakfast at one point or another.) Its creator, Majed Ali, strives to make Middle Eastern recipes approachable to an international audience. This tart, similar to a cheesecake that lost some of its sweetness but kept all the richness, is the gateway recipe you'll wish you'd known about years ago.

1. Preheat the oven to 350°F. In a food processor, process granola, salt, sugar, and cinnamon until fine. Add melted butter and process until well combined.

2. Press the mixture firmly into the bottom and sides of a 9-inch tart pan. Bake for 8 minutes, remove from oven, and reduce oven temperature to 300°F.

3. In a bowl, whisk eggs, lime zest, vanilla, sea salt, and granulated sugar until combined. Fold in labneh, but do not overmix. Pour the filling gently into the tart shell and spread evenly.

3. Bake for 18 to 23 minutes, until edges are set and the center wobbles slightly when pan is gently shaken. Turn off the oven and leave the door ajar to let tart cool for an hour. Remove from oven and let cool to room temperature for 3 hours.

4. To make the honey lime syrup, bring lime juice and honey to a boil in a small saucepan for 1 minute. Remove from heat and allow to cool. Top the tart with strawberries and drizzle on honey lime syrup.

Chocolate Caramel Tart

Erica Leahy, Three Daughters Baking in Maplewood, NJ

Makes one 10-inch tart

For the chocolate tart dough:

⅞ cup (1 stick + 6 tablespoons) butter

¼ teaspoon salt

1⅛ cups powdered sugar

1 egg

2¼ cups all-purpose flour

½ cup Dutch-processed cocoa powder

For the caramel filling:

1 cup granulated sugar

½ cup water, optional

2 tablespoons corn syrup

½ cup cream

¼ cup (½ stick) butter

2 tablespoons sour cream

½ teaspoon salt

1 teaspoon vanilla extract

For the chocolate caramel ganache:

1 cup sugar

½ cup water, optional

1 cup cream

8 ounces milk chocolate

4 ounces bittersweet chocolate (53%–64%)

3 tablespoons butter, softened

1 teaspoon salt

2 teaspoons vanilla extract

pinch of sea salt, for garnish

This tart will make you wish you were a miniature person so you could dive into its viscous basin of silken caramel and splash around; maybe do some laps or the backstroke under its dark chocolate roof. Yep, there you are, just paddling around with your itty-bitty body in your sweet, creamy lagoon. Alas, you can't swim in this tart, but you can eat it, which is better than being a miniature person anyway. Or at least I assume it is, because I'm not miniature and can't fully know for sure.

1. In a stand mixer fitted with the paddle attachment, cream the butter and salt together until smooth and no chunks of butter remain. Add powdered sugar and mix to combine. Scrape down the bowl.

2. Add egg and thoroughly mix. Scrape down the bowl and paddle. On low speed, add the flour and cocoa powder and mix to combine.

3. Remove from mixer and scrape dough onto a work surface. Press the dough into a disc and wrap in plastic. Refrigerate for 20 to 30 minutes.

4. On a lightly floured surface, roll the dough into a 12-inch disc, approximately ⅛-inch thick. Transfer the dough to a 10-inch tart pan with removable bottom. Press dough into bottom and up the sides. Trim excess and reserve for another use.

5. Preheat the oven to 375°F. Dock, or prick, the bottom of the tart with a fork and refrigerate for 30 minutes.

6. Bake the tart shell for 20 minutes, or until it is thoroughly dry. If the dough bubbles during baking, use the back of a measuring cup to gently press flat. Set aside to cool completely.

7. For the caramel filling: In a medium saucepan, combine the sugar, water (if using), and corn syrup. Cook over high heat until it's a deep amber color.

8. Turn off the heat and whisk in the cream, butter, and sour cream. Add these ingredients carefully so as not to splatter, and use a long-handled whisk. Once thoroughly mixed, add the salt and vanilla. Set aside to cool.

9. For the ganache: In a medium saucepan, cook the sugar and water (if using) to a deep amber color. Turn off the heat and carefully stir in the cream.

10. Measure your milk and dark chocolates into a mixing bowl. Once the caramel mixture has stopped bubbling, gently pour it over the chocolate. Gently stir to thoroughly combine. Add in the softened butter, salt, and vanilla. Stir gently until you have a smooth ganache. Set aside.

11. To assemble, remove the cooled tart shell from the pan. Pour the caramel mixture into the bottom of the shell so there is about ¼ inch of caramel. (You can keep the rest for something else.) Chill the tart for 20 minutes to set the caramel. After the caramel is set, gently pour the ganache over the top to fill the tart shell. Allow the tart to set, and sprinkle the top with a pinch of sea salt before serving.

Peanut Butter Pie

Kelli Marks, Sweet Love Bakes in Little Rock, AR

Makes one 10-inch pie

For the crust:

½ cup (1 stick) unsalted butter, softened

½ cup granulated sugar

½ cup Dutch-processed cocoa

¼ teaspoon salt

¼ teaspoon baking powder

1 large egg

1¼ cups all-purpose flour

For the coating:

¼ cup heavy whipping cream

⅓ cup dark chocolate

For the filling:

2 cups heavy whipping cream

8 ounces mascarpone

1 cup creamy peanut butter

1 teaspoon salt

1 teaspoon vanilla

1½ cups powdered sugar

chopped peanut butter cups, for topping (optional)

It's not just a dessert; it's a state of mind. A peanut butter pie state of mind. A salty, sweet, creamy, bitter, rich mood that transcends calories and mascarpone and becomes a state unto itself. Because that's what happens when peanut butter filling meets cocoa cookie crust—consciousnesses are cracked, and days are made.

1. Preheat the oven to 350°F. In a medium bowl, combine butter, sugar, cocoa, salt, and baking powder. Use a hand mixer or stand mixer fitted with the paddle attachment.

2. Scrape down sides and add the egg; mix until combined. Add the flour in two batches.

3. Once combined, press into the bottom and sides of a 10-inch pie pan. (If you only have a 9-inch, don't use all of the dough; it will be too thick. Only use as much as you need to cover a ¼-inch thickness on the bottom and sides.) Bake for 20 minutes. The sides will be puffy and the bottom will no longer appear glossy. Use a measuring cup to gently press the bottom and sides down. Set the crust aside and allow to cool.

4. In a microwave-safe bowl, combine the dark chocolate and heavy cream and heat for 30-second intervals until completely melted. Pour into the bottom of the crust.

5. In a stand mixer fitted with the whisk attachment or in a large bowl using a hand mixer, whip the heavy cream until stiff peaks are achieved. Set this aside.

6. Still using your stand mixer or hand mixer, combine mascarpone, peanut butter, salt, and vanilla and whip until fluffy. Add powdered sugar to the mixture in three batches. Mix until combined, scraping down sides as necessary. Fold in the reserved whipped cream by hand.

7. Pour filling into cooled crust and top with chopped peanut butter cups if desired. Allow to chill 2 hours before serving.

Blueberry Galette

Jennifer Essex, owner of Ruby Jean Patisserie in Denver, CO

Makes one galette

For the crust:

1⅞ cups all-purpose flour

½ teaspoon salt

⅔ cups (1 stick + 3 tablespoons) unsalted butter, cubed and cold

⅓ cup water, very cold

Turbinado sugar, for sprinkling

For the filling:

2 cups fresh or frozen blueberries

⅛ cup sugar

pinch of salt

½ teaspoon vanilla

1 tablespoon fresh lemon juice

4 tablespoons cornstarch

God bless the galette. Less fussy but just as stunning as an intricate pie, the galette is a free-form pastry, which means if it doesn't turn out the way you intended, you can totally claim artistic license. There's *almost* no messing it up, which is probably why "galette fails" has only 291,000 Google results while "pie fails" has more than 31 million. (Yes, I looked it up.) Galette: easier than pie.

1. For the crust, mix salt and flour. Using a bench cutter or knives, cut in butter into the flour/salt mixture until butter pieces are pea-sized.

2. Mix in water and knead quickly. Add more flour if mixture is too wet, or more water if too dry. Shape into a disk, wrap in plastic, and chill for at least 2 hours.

3. Combine all filling ingredients in a bowl. Roll your pie dough into a 12-inch round circle.

4. Line a baking sheet with parchment paper and place dough onto the sheet. Put the fruit filling in the center of dough, leaving a 2-inch rim. Pile fruit high and crimp dough edges. Freeze for 45 minutes.

5. Preheat the oven to 375°F. Egg wash the folded sides of the galette and sprinkle with Turbinado sugar.

6. Bake for 1 hour (or longer), checking for a brown and crisp crust. Let rest for 30 minutes, then you're free to serve with vanilla ice cream.

CHAPTER 4

Things You Eat with Your Hands

CHEWY BROWNIES 99
Tessa Arias, baking blogger (*Handle the Heat*)

CHOCOLATE BABKA 100
Duff Goldman, owner of Charm City Cakes

CROISSANTS 102
Dominique Ansel, chef/owner of Dominique Ansel Bakery in New York, NY

LEMON BARS 107
Ashley Summers, Executive Pastry Chef, Berkshire Bakes in Pittsfield, MA

BLONDIE ATE A BROWNIE 110
Sherry Blockinger, pastry chef/founder of Sherry B Dessert Studio

PISTACHIO CHEESECAKE BARS 113
Katina Talley, owner of Sweet Magnolias Bake Shop in Omaha, NE

CHOCOLATE CHEESECAKE MOCHI MUFFINS 114
Sam Butarbutar, cofounder and culinary director of Third Culture Bakery in Aurora, CO and Berkeley, CA

SALTED CARAMEL BROWNIES 117
Kimberlee Ho, baking blogger (*Kickass Baker*)

PEACH COBBLER SCONES 118
Rebecca Rather, Emma + Ollie in Fredericksburg, TX

BISCOFF WHITE CHOCOLATE BLONDIES 121
Anna Wierzbinska, baking blogger (*Anna Banana*)

Chewy Brownies

Tessa Arias, baking blogger (*Handle the Heat*)

Makes one 8x8-inch pan

- 1¼ cups granulated sugar
- 5 tablespoons unsalted butter
- 2 large eggs plus 1 egg yolk, cold
- 1 teaspoon vanilla extract
- ⅓ cup vegetable oil
- ¾ cup unsweetened cocoa powder
- ½ cup all-purpose flour
- ⅛ teaspoon baking soda
- 1 tablespoon cornstarch
- ¼ teaspoon salt
- ¾ cup semisweet chocolate chips

I think it's safe to say that Tessa Arias is a brownie geek. She's published 40 brownie recipes on her blog, *Handle the Heat*, and she spends her free time doing things like experimenting with cornstarch amounts and egg yolk temperatures. We're grateful for her efforts because they've yielded us these incredible, one-bowl, so much better-than-the-box, chewy brownies. (Seriously: one bowl!) We're talking wall-to-wall chocolate action, where every bite is jammed with fudgy goodness and chocolate chips. And did I mention you can do it all in one bowl? There may be no greater reward-to-effort ratio.

1. Preheat the oven to 325°F. Line an 8x8-inch pan with foil and spray with nonstick cooking spray.

2. In a microwave-safe bowl, add the butter and sugar. Microwave for about 1 minute, or until the butter is melted. Whisk in the eggs, egg yolk, and vanilla. Stir in the oil and cocoa powder.

3. With a rubber spatula, stir in the flour, baking soda, cornstarch, and salt until combined. Stir in the chocolate chips.

4. Spread the brownie batter evenly into the prepared pan. Place in the oven and bake for 30 minutes, or until the brownies are set and a toothpick inserted in the center has moist crumbs attached. Do not overcook. Let cool completely before cutting and serving.

Chocolate Babka

Duff Goldman, owner of Charm City Cakes in Baltimore, MD, and Los Angeles, CA

Makes two loaves

For the dough:

1 ¼-ounce packet active dry yeast

½ cup whole milk, at room temperature

⅓ cup sugar, plus a pinch

4½ cups all-purpose flour, plus more for dusting

4 large eggs

1½ teaspoons kosher salt

1 teaspoon pure vanilla extract

½ teaspoon ground nutmeg

1 teaspoon grated lemon zest

10 tablespoons unsalted butter, at room temperature

For the filling:

½ cup sugar

¾ cup heavy cream

pinch of kosher salt

1 cup bittersweet chocolate chips

1 stick unsalted butter, cut into pieces, at room temperature

2 teaspoons pure vanilla extract

For the topping:

½ cup all-purpose flour

3 tablespoons sugar

1 tablespoon unsweetened cocoa powder

pinch of kosher salt

4 tablespoons unsalted butter, at room temperature

⅓ cup mini chocolate chips

Babka means "little grandmother" in many eastern European countries, so it's only fitting that Duff Goldman's recipe for this sweet, buttery, chocolate babka comes from his maternal great-grandmother, Esther Steinberg. The bread-cake takes some patience to make. There's yeast involved, so it needs time to do its puffing, swelling thing—but the swirly, gooey slices are so worth it that you'll see why Esther was known as the "Ace of Babkas" in her stomping grounds of Wichita, Kansas.

1. Make the dough: Sprinkle the yeast over the milk in a liquid measuring cup; add a pinch of sugar and set aside until bubbly, about 7 minutes. Combine the flour, the remaining ⅓ cup sugar, the eggs, yeast mixture, salt, vanilla, nutmeg, and lemon zest in a large bowl. Stir with a wooden spoon to combine. Turn the dough out onto a work surface and knead until soft and smooth, about 5 minutes. Knead in the butter in three additions, dusting the dough with flour if it's too sticky. Transfer the dough to a large bowl; cover with plastic wrap and let rise at room temperature, about 1 ½ hours. Punch down the dough, re-cover with plastic wrap, and let rise in the fridge overnight.

2. Make the filling: Heat the sugar, heavy cream and salt in a saucepan until scalding. Pour over the bittersweet chocolate chips, butter, and vanilla in a bowl. Whisk until smooth and shiny. Let cool to room temperature.

3. Make the topping: Whisk the flour, sugar, cocoa powder, and salt in a separate bowl; work in the butter with your fingers until the mixture is sandy and chunky. Stir in the mini chocolate chips; set the topping aside.

4. Form the loaves: Cut the dough in half with a bench scraper or chef's knife. Using a rolling pin, roll each half into a 12-by-16-inch rectangle. Using an offset spatula, spread the filling on both dough rectangles, all the way to the edges. Starting from a long side, tightly roll each rectangle into a log. Wrap each log in plastic wrap and refrigerate 15 minutes. Unwrap the logs; cut each in half lengthwise with a bench scraper or chef's knife. Twist the halves together a few times, starting from the middle. Coat two 9-by-5-inch loaf pans with cooking spray and line with parchment, then spray the parchment. Place a dough twist snugly in each pan. Cover with plastic wrap and let rise 1 ½ hours.

5. Finish and bake the babka: Preheat the oven to 350°F. Brush each loaf with butter and sprinkle with the topping. Bake until browned, about 45 minutes. Meanwhile, make some simple syrup: Combine the sugar and water in a saucepan; simmer, stirring, until the sugar dissolves. Let cool. Pull the loaves out of the oven and immediately

For finishing:

cooking spray

**4 tablespoons unsalted butter,
at room temperature**

¾ cup sugar

¾ cup water

poke a bunch of holes in each with a
wooden skewer. Pour 1¼ cups simple
syrup evenly over the loaves.

6. Let sit 10 minutes, then remove
the babka from the pans, remove the
parchment, and let cool completely on
a rack.

Croissants

Dominique Ansel, chef/owner of Dominique Ansel Bakery in New York, NY

Makes 15 croissants

For the dough:

6½ cups bread flour

2½ teaspoons salt

⅓ cup sugar

¼ cup fresh yeast

5 teaspoons honey

⅓ cup butter, room temperature

⅗ cup water

¾ cup milk

1 large egg

For the butter block:

2 cups (4 sticks) butter, room temperature

For the egg wash:

1 large egg

1 teaspoon milk

¼ teaspoon salt

We can't really talk about Dominique Ansel without mentioning the C-word. I mean, the man's baked goods stopped traffic, inspired an underground pastry economy, and created a full-on cultural phenomenon, but Dominique's penchant for patisserie extends well beyond the Cronut.® He says he still works every day to perfect his croissant. (Although the hordes of people lining up outside his bakeries would argue that they're already pretty darn perfect.)

Although making the flaky little crescents is an advanced process, Dominique has simplified it for us a bit here, and, in fact, this is the recipe he uses at home. "Croissants can seem intimidating to many people as it can get technical," he says. "Small changes in humidity, temperature, and time can cause some pretty large variances and truthfully, it's a lifelong study. But my advice is to still try. It is a win-win situation when even the imperfect croissants still taste delicious, warm and just baked." So go forward with your croissant efforts, and delight in the perfectly imperfect.

1. To make the dough: In a stand mixer fitted with a dough hook, add in all your ingredients for the dough, putting in the dry ingredients first, then adding in the wet. Mix on slow speed until everything is incorporated, about 2 to 3 minutes. Then switch to mix on high speed until the dough is smooth with a little bit of elasticity, about 5 to 7 minutes.

2. Remove the dough from the mixer bowl and place on a flat working surface. Using your palms, tightly roll the dough into a ball so it becomes smooth and firm. If you press your finger deep into the dough, it should spring back. Once the dough is firm, use a knife to cut an "X" in the top. Then spread open the edges so it forms a square. Place the dough on a half sheet tray lined with parchment paper. Lightly cover the top of the dough with plastic wrap.

3. For the first fermentation, leave the covered dough out in a warm part of the room (i.e. near the oven) and let it proof until it has roughly doubled or almost tripled in size, about 2 hours. Once it has proofed, press down the dough with your palms until it is flat and no longer has air. Straighten out the sides with your palms so it stays roughly the shape of a 7-inch square. Place the dough, still covered in plastic wrap pressed to the surface, in the refrigerator.

4. To make the butter block, place your room temperature butter in between two sheets of parchment paper. Using the palm of your hand, press down on the butter to flatten. Use a dough scraper to help straighten out the edges so that you form roughly a 7-inch square that is about ⅛-inch thick. Place your butter block in the refrigerator, still in between the 2 parchment pieces.

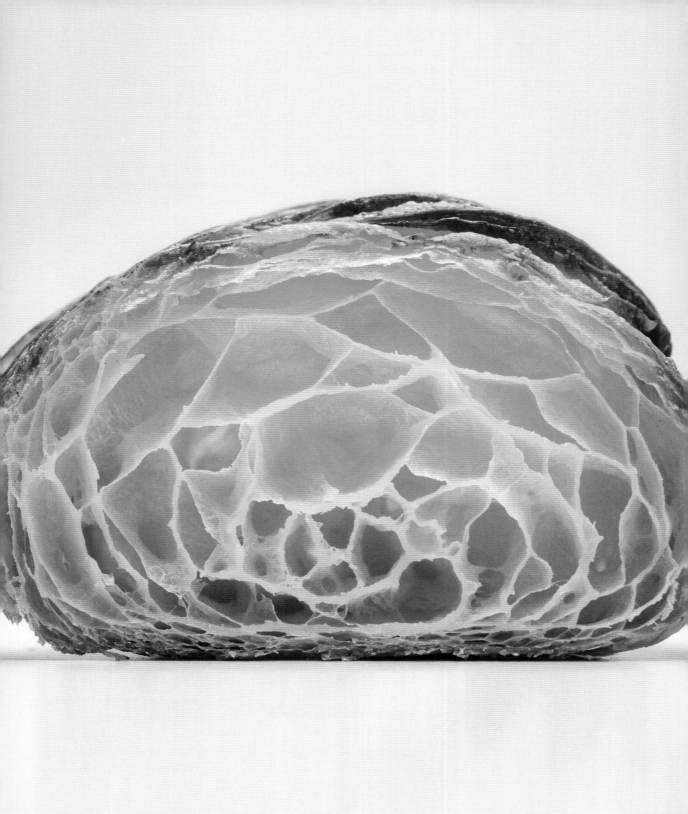

5. After about 1 hour in the refrigerator, the dough will go through a second fermentation and proof slightly (but not double in volume). Press it down once again. Let the dough and butter block rest in the refrigerator overnight so that it can relax and be easier to laminate the next day.

6. For lamination: Once the dough and butter block have rested overnight, remove both from the refrigerator. The dough should be as cold as possible (even if it needs a few minutes in the freezer). The butter block, on the other hand, may need to sit out for a few minutes so that it can slightly temper and bend without cracking. When the temperature of the dough and butter are right, you can begin to laminate. Lightly dust a flat surface with flour. Unwrap the dough and place it on the surface. You may want to lightly roll it out into the size of a 7-inch square if it has shrunk overnight. (As you roll, don't forget to slide the dough, adding more flour to the table as needed so it does not stick.) Arrange the butter block in the center of the dough so it looks like a diamond in the center of the square (rotated 45 degrees, with the corners of the butter block facing the center of the dough sides). Pull the corners of the dough up and over to the center of the butter block until you've wrapped up the butter block completely. Pinch the seams of the dough together to fully seal the butter inside. You should have a packet of dough and butter that is a slightly larger square at 7 to 8 inches.

7. With a rolling pin, using steady and even pressure, roll the croissant dough so that it quadruples in length. When finished you should have a rectangle that is roughly 28 inches long, 10 inches wide, and ¼ inch thick. Place the dough so the longer side runs left to right. Fold the right side in just a bit before the center of the dough, keeping the edges lined up. Fold the left side over to meet the right side. Then fold in half again. This is called a "double" or "book" fold because it closes up like a book. Wrap the dough in plastic wrap and place it in the refrigerator for 25 to 30 minutes.

8. Remove the croissant dough from the refrigerator, unwrap, and place it on a lightly floured surface. Orient the dough so the seam is always on the right side (and the "opening" is on the top and bottom). Roll the dough out vertically again from the top to the bottom until it has tripled in length. When finished, you should have a rectangle that is roughly 21 inches long, 10 inches wide, and ¼ inch thick. Orient the dough so the longer side runs left to right. From the right side, fold ⅓ of the dough onto itself, keeping the edges lined up with each other. From the left side, fold the remaining ⅓ of the dough on top of the side already folded. Line up all the edges so you are left again with a square. This is called a "letter" or "single" fold because it is how you would fold a letter to place inside an envelope. Wrap the dough in plastic wrap and let it rest again in the refrigerator for 25 to 30 minutes.

9. Now it's time for the final sheeting. Remove the croissant dough from the refrigerator, unwrap, and place it on a lightly floured surface. Orient your dough so the seam is on the right and the "opening" is on the top and bottom. Roll out the croissant dough again lengthwise to roughly triple in length, or a rectangle that is 24 inches long, 10 inches wide, and ¼ inch thick.

10. Cutting a croissant: With the long end of the dough running left to right, it's now time to cut your croissant. Trim the top and bottom of the dough so it is in a straight line. With a ruler, measure one side of an isosceles triangle that is roughly 10½ inches and cut with a large knife. Next, measure out the base of the triangle, which should be 3 inches wide. Now cut the third side of the triangle. This will be the triangle for your regular croissant. To make it easier, you can make a mark every 3 inches and cut the remaining dough into isosceles triangles.

11. Place the cut dough pieces on top of a parchment-lined half sheet tray and put it back into the refrigerator to chill for 10 to 15 minutes, loosely covered in plastic wrap.

12. Get ready to roll your croissants! Remove the croissant triangles from the refrigerator. Holding onto the wider base with one hand, use the other hand's thumb and index finger to gently pull the dough to stretch and relax it. It should be 2 inches or so longer. Orient the base of the triangle toward you and slowly roll up from the base to the tip gently without being too tight.

13. Line a half sheet tray with parchment paper. It's time to "tray up" the croissants and prepare them for proofing and baking. Place the croissants with their "tails" at the bottom of the tray so they do not unravel, and space each croissant at least 2 to 3 inches apart from the sides and each other. As a tip, use a small cosmetic spray bottle and spray a little water over the surface of the croissant dough to prevent it forming a skin on top as they proof. Lightly cover with plastic wrap. Let proof at a bit warmer than room temperature (roughly 80°F), until they double or almost triple in size, 2 to 3 hours.

14. Preheat the oven to 400°F. Whisk together the egg, milk, and salt to make the egg wash. Once your croissants have proofed, lightly use a pastry brush to brush a thin, even layer over the top of the croissants.

15. Bake for approximately 20 minutes until golden brown, and the dough is no longer wet. Eat and enjoy! Croissants are best consumed the same day they are baked, within 6 to 8 hours. If cutting, please use a serrated knife to avoid crushing the layers.

Lemon Bars

Ashley Summers, executive pastry chef, Berkshire Bakes in Pittsfield, MA

Makes one 8x8-inch pan

For the crust:

1 cup all-purpose flour

½ teaspoon kosher salt

⅓ cup powdered sugar

½ cup (1 stick) butter, cold

1 teaspoon vanilla extract

1 egg white (save from separated yolks below for filling)

For the filling:

1¼ cups sugar

2 tablespoons cornstarch

¼ teaspoon kosher salt

⅔ cup fresh lemon juice (3 to 4 lemons)

zest from 1 lemon

2 eggs

4 egg yolks

6 tablespoons butter

powdered sugar, for topping

I'd say that these zingy little quadrilaterals are bake sale-worthy, but I don't think you're going to want to part with them, even if it is for a good cause. (Does your kid's school really need more computers?) These guys are just so sunny and spunky that they'll make you want to break out in song, but you won't because your mouth is full of their tangy lemon curd filling and buttery shortbread crust and you can't risk losing a single morsel by belting out an ode to their confection perfection. Just keep on chewing and not contributing anything to your kid's bake sale.

1. Preheat the oven to 350°F. Pan spray an 8x8-inch glass baking dish and line it with two strips of parchment paper (8x12-inch), crossed. The extra parchment paper will help you easily lift the bars from the dish once cooled.

2. For the crust, add flour, salt, and powdered sugar to a bowl. Cut the cold butter into quarters the long way and then dice to get small squares of butter. With a pastry cutter or in a food processor, work the butter into the dry ingredients until butter is coated and pea-sized.

3. Add the vanilla and give the dough one more pulse or mix until it balls up into quarter-sized dough pebbles. Lightly push the dough into the prepared pan and bake for 12 to 15 minutes, until lightly brown but not quite golden. Overbaking the crust can prevent the lemon layer from sticking to the crust once cooled.

4. Remove from oven and, while hot, lightly brush egg white across the crust a few times. The white should cook immediately and form a thin, glossy layer over the crust. This will act as a barrier and keep your crust from getting soggy. While hot, poke all over with a fork. This will release any steam and keep your crust crisp and buttery.

5. For the filling, mix together sugar, cornstarch, and salt. Add in fresh lemon juice and zest. Whisk in eggs and yolks.

6. Transfer to a heavy-bottomed pot over medium to low heat, whisking continuously until it turns from a liquid to a soft pudding-like consistency. Remove from heat, continue whisking, and add in butter.

7. Strain filling directly on top of the crust and bake for 8 to 12 minutes. The top should wiggle slightly and should not stick to your finger when lightly touched. Cool completely before lifting from pan and slicing. Rinse knife after each slice to keep sides of bar looking clean. Sprinkle generously with powdered sugar.

Blondie Ate a Brownie

Sherry Blockinger, *pastry chef/founder of Sherry B Dessert Studio*

Makes about 18 bars

12 ounces semisweet chocolate, chopped or chips

1 14-ounce can sweetened condensed milk

2 tablespoons unsalted butter (European-style recommended)

1 cup (2 sticks) unsalted butter, melted

2¼ cups packed light brown sugar (1 pound)

2 large eggs

1 teaspoon kosher salt

1 cup pecans, chopped

¾ cup flaked sweetened coconut

1 teaspoon pure vanilla extract

2 cups unbleached all-purpose flour

Nostalgia is a taste, and if you don't believe me, well, I'm sorry about your childhood and hopefully you have a good therapist. But if you know the sweet, sweet wistfulness that is biting into something that has you both pining for and celebrating something that was and never will be again, then yay! You know the punch of nostalgia. Sherry Blockinger's slabs of blondies blanketing a fudgy brownie taste like this happiness-meets-homesick feeling, so it's no surprise that the bars were inspired by her family's recipe from the 1970s.

1. Preheat the oven to 350°F. Grab a 9x13x2-inch ungreased baking pan. (Hint: if you line the pan with foil or parchment leaving an overhang on the sides and spray with nonstick spray, you can lift the whole blondie out of the pan before cutting.)

2. Combine the chocolate, condensed milk, and the 2 tablespoons of butter in a separate pan or ovenproof dish. Place in the oven to melt, or melt over a double boiler. Stir to combine. Set aside to cool.

3. In a large mixing bowl, blend the melted butter, sugar, eggs, salt, pecans, coconut, vanilla, and flour. Mix well. (But try not to incorporate too much air when mixing.)

4. Spread half of the dough in a thin layer to just cover the bottom of the pan. Completely cover the dough with the chocolate mixture, spreading evenly to the ends. Cover the chocolate layer with the balance of the dough and spread evenly. Bake for 30 to 35 minutes until golden brown on the edges and set in the middle; rotate halfway through baking to guarantee even color and doneness. Let cool and cut into bars.

Pistachio Cheesecake Bars

Katina Talley, owner of Sweet Magnolias Bake Shop in Omaha, NE

Makes enough for one 9x13-inch pan, about 15 bars

For the crust:

6 tablespoons (¾ stick) unsalted butter

1½ cups graham crackers, finely ground

1½ cups all-purpose flour

½ cup light brown sugar

For the cheesecake:

¾ cup pistachios

24 ounces cream cheese, room temperature

1 cup granulated sugar

3 eggs

1½ teaspoons almond extract

¼ teaspoon salt

¾ cup sour cream

¾ cup heavy whipping cream

green food coloring, if desired (gel works best)

For the honey cream topping:

½ cup sour cream

2 tablespoons honey

½ teaspoon vanilla

additional chopped pistachios and bee pollen, for garnish (optional)

I'm just gonna say it: Pistachio and cream cheese is the most underrated flavor combination on the planet. I love chocolate and peanut butter as much as the next mom stealing her kid's Reese's out of the Halloween bag while they sleep, but pistachio and cream cheese is a whole other level of flavors uniting for dreamy results. Rich with salty; creamy with crunchy—it just *works*, and these bars from Sweet Magnolias Bake Shop prove it. Add the graham cracker streusel-esque crust and a dollop of honey cream on top, and you might even forget Reese's exist (at least for as long as you're gnawing on these beauties).

1. Preheat the oven to 350°F. Grease a 9x13-inch pan with cooking spray, line with parchment paper, and grease parchment again with cooking spray.

2. In a microwave-safe bowl, melt butter. In a mixing bowl, whisk together the ground graham crackers, flour, and brown sugar. Create a well and pour in the melted butter. Fold together until well mixed.

3. Press firmly and evenly into prepared pan for desired amount of crust. Bake for 16 to 18 minutes. Allow to cool while preparing the cheesecake.

4. Using a food processor, grind pistachios into the texture of coarse sand. The finer the better, and the smoother your bars will turn out. Using a stand mixer fitted with the paddle attachment, whip the cream cheese on medium-high speed until smooth. Add sugar to the bowl and mix on medium until well blended. Next, add eggs one at a time, making sure to scrape the bottom and sides of the bowl after each addition. Stir in almond extract and salt.

5. When your mixture is smooth, add sour cream and heavy whipping cream and mix until combined. Stir in pistachios and adjust color with food coloring if desired.

6. Spread cheesecake mixture on top of the cooled graham cracker crust. Make sure to spread evenly and to reach the corners. Bake for 30 to 35 minutes until set (center will still jiggle slightly). Chill completely before cutting into bars and serving.

7. To make the honey cream topping, stir sour cream, honey, and vanilla in a small mixing bowl. Once cooled and cut, dollop each bar with about a tablespoon of honey cream. If you're an overachiever, sprinkle with coarsely chopped pistachios and bee pollen.

Chocolate Cheesecake Mochi Muffins

Sam Butarbutar, cofounder and culinary director of Third
Culture Bakery in Aurora, CO and Berkeley, CA

Makes a dozen muffins

For the chocolate batter:

½ cup cocoa powder
(natural, not Dutched)

1½ cups whole milk

1¾ cups dark chocolate
chips or disks (60%–68%)

3 eggs, room temperature

7 tablespoons butter, melted

2 teaspoons vanilla extract

1½ cups mochiko rice flour

1⅔ cups cane sugar

1 teaspoon baking powder

1 teaspoon kosher salt

For the cream cheese batter:

1 cup cream cheese,
room temperature

¼ cup + 1 teaspoon cane sugar

1 egg, room temperature

1 teaspoon vanilla extract

2 teaspoons fresh lemon juice

handful of Maldon/flaky
sea salt, for sprinkling

Don't let the mochiko rice flour intimidate you—once you score some from your local Asian market (or Amazon) these chocolate cheesecake muffins are so easy to make. The Mochi Muffins® that Sam Butarbutar and his husband Wenter Shyu make at their Third Culture Bakeries are inspired by their childhoods in Indonesia and Taiwan, but this particular flavor comes from Sam's obsession with everything chocolate and everything cheesecake.

The mochi rice flour gives the muffins a fudgy, chewier texture, which means that more will end up in your mouth instead of in a crumbly mess on the floor, as is often the tragedy with traditional muffins. And as the floor does not deserve the goodness that is these chocolate cheesecake mochi muffins, this is a win. You deserve this goodness, so go get that mochiko rice flour and enjoy your fudgier, chewier, less crumbly muffins already.

1. Preheat the oven to 350°F (or 300°F if using convection oven). Really butter your muffin pan, making sure to hit every nook and cranny.

2. In a medium pot, place cocoa powder and whole milk. Cook over medium-high heat and continually whisk to get rid of lumps. The mixture has to boil to cook away the "raw" taste of the cocoa powder. Once it boils, remove from heat and add the chocolate chips/disks. Whisk until melted and smooth.

3. Add eggs, butter, and vanilla to the pot and whisk until combined. In the same pot, add all the dry ingredients and stir until combined. Set aside.

4. In a medium bowl, add all of the cream cheese batter ingredients and whisk with a balloon whisk until smooth.

5. Use a small scooper or spoon to fill the muffin wells halfway full of the chocolate batter. Then add about 2 tablespoons of the cream cheese batter to each well. Top each well with more chocolate batter. You'll want the batter to fill all the way to the rim of the well. Sprinkle lightly with your flaky sea salt.

6. Bake for 45 to 50 minutes. You'll know they're done when a toothpick comes out mostly clean. Let cool completely in the pan for about an hour. Resist the urge to eat them when they're warm—the chocolate and cheesecake need this time to finish cooking and do their magic. Once completely cooled, remove from pans and enjoy! They'll last 2 to 3 days at room temperature; do not refrigerate.

Salted Caramel Brownies

Kimberlee Ho, baking blogger (*Kickass Baker*)

*Makes 16 giant, super
fudgy brownies*

For the salted caramel:

½ cup granulated sugar

3 tablespoons salted butter,
room temperature, cubed

¼ cup heavy cream

½ teaspoon kosher salt

For the brownies:

6 ounces unsweetened
baking chocolate bar

1 cup (2 sticks) salted butter

4 large eggs

2 cups granulated sugar

1 tablespoon vanilla extract

¾ cup all-purpose flour

1 cup caramel, butterscotch,
chocolate or pretty much
whatever chips you've got

flaky sea salt

When we add chocolate to the holy trinity that is butter, sugar, and flour, good things happen. When we add salted caramel to that quaternity (yes, that's a word; I looked it up), even better things happen—namely, Kimberlee Ho's salted caramel brownies.

These monstrously thick, fudgy squares, stuffed with butterscotch chips (or whatever you have on hand) and topped with salty, melted caramel, are so beautifully chewy and chocolatey that you will want to set up camp amidst their rich, gooey crumbs. But you can't do that because humans can't live inside brownies, so instead you will have to merely eat them, which is almost as good as living in them.

1. Line an 8x8-inch baking pan with parchment paper. In a medium saucepan, start the salted caramel by heating the sugar over medium heat, stirring constantly. It will melt into an amber-colored liquid as you heat and stir it. Once the sugar is melted, add butter (careful; it may splatter!) and whisk until fully incorporated. Slowly drizzle in the heavy cream while stirring the mixture. Boil for a minute, then remove from heat and add salt. Pour into prepared pan and place in the freezer for 20 to 30 minutes.

2. Preheat the oven to 350°F, and line a second 8x8-inch pan with parchment paper. (Or remove the caramel once it's firm, and re-use that pan.) Melt the chocolate and butter in a saucepan over medium-low heat.

3. Meanwhile, in the bowl of a stand mixer, beat the eggs on medium speed until light yellow, about 5 minutes. Add sugar and blend on low until combined.

4. Add vanilla and melted chocolate to the egg and sugar mixture. Add flour and beat until smooth. Stir in caramel chips.

5. Pour batter into prepared pan. If you haven't already, remove caramel from freezer and lift parchment out of pan. Cut into squares. Place the caramel squares on top of the brownie batter, spreading evenly over surface. (Don't use them all, though, you'll want more for the end.)

6. Bake 45 to 55 minutes (or longer—these things are huge!), until toothpick inserted in center comes out clean. Cool to room temperature, then cover and refrigerate for at least an hour. Warm the remaining salted caramel and spread over the top. Sprinkle with sea salt and cut into 16 squares.

Peach Cobbler Scones

Rebecca Rather, Emma + Ollie in Fredericksburg, TX

Makes 6+ scones

For the crumble:

1 cup flour

1 cup sugar

pinch of salt

½ cup (1 stick) butter, cut into cubes

For the scones:

4 cups unbleached all-purpose flour

1 cup sugar

1 tablespoon baking powder

½ teaspoon baking soda

½ teaspoon kosher salt

1 cup (2 sticks) cold unsalted butter, cut into cubes

1 cup fresh peaches, cut into cubes

1 cup cream

1 cup buttermilk

Rebecca Rather has three cookbooks called "The Pastry Queen," and scones are one of the queen's specialties—which pretty much makes these peach cobbler scones royalty. It may sound a little morbid to want to eat royalty, but that's exactly what you're going to want to do to these peachy, crumble-topped, majestic scones. If scones make you contemplative, maybe take a moment to mull over the monarchy's relevance in 21st-century life before bowing down to the scones' impossibly fluffy grandness.

1. Preheat the oven to 375°F. Make the crumble by mixing flour, sugar, and salt together in the bowl of an electric mixer fitted with the paddle attachment. Add butter and mix until the mixture looks dry and crumbly.

2. Line a baking sheet with parchment paper. Mix flour, sugar, baking powder, baking soda, and salt together in a large bowl.

3. Add the butter and gradually cut it in with a pastry blender or two knives until mixture resembles small peas.

4. Add peaches, cream, and buttermilk and mix by hand just until all the ingredients are incorporated. If the dough is too dry to hold together, add more buttermilk.

5. Divide the dough into 6 (or more, depending on how big you want them) equal pieces and place on baking sheet. Sprinkle the crumble on top of each scone and bake for 12 to 15 minutes, or until firm to the touch.

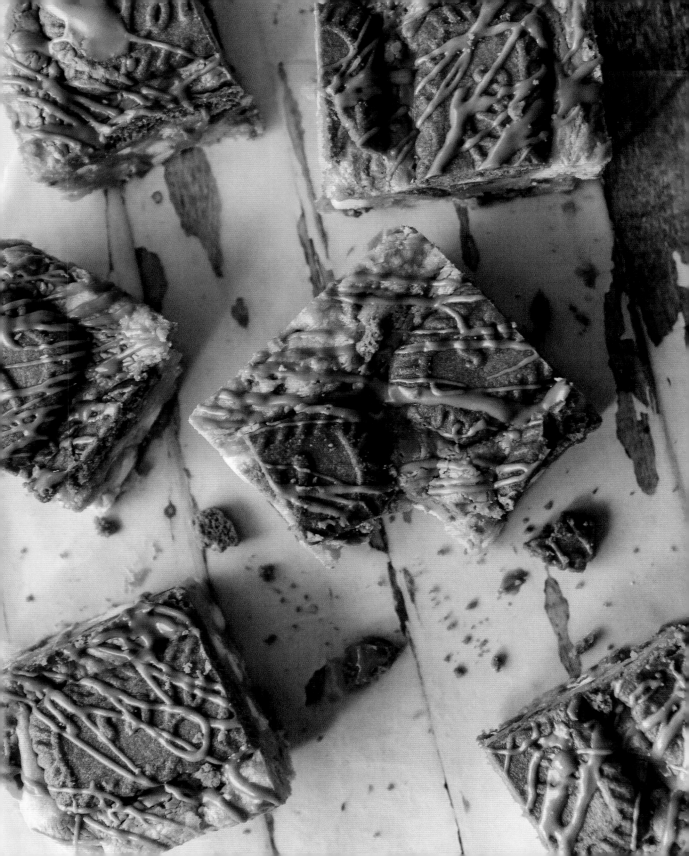

Biscoff White Chocolate Blondies

Anna Wierzbinska, baking blogger (*Anna Banana*)

*Makes one 9x9-inch pan,
or about 9 pieces*

**About ½ of an 8.8-ounce package
Biscoff cookies (16 cookies)**

**1 cup (2 sticks) unsalted
butter, softened**

**½ cup + 1 tablespoon
caster sugar**

½ cup light brown sugar

2 teaspoons vanilla

2 large eggs, room temperature

2 cups + 1 tablespoon flour

1 teaspoon salt

**5½ ounces (or just over 1 cup)
chopped white chocolate**

**3 tablespoons Biscoff
cookie butter spread**

Brit Anna Wierzbinska calls this "a corker of a recipe" (I think that means really, really good); I call her Biscoff white chocolate blondies the best way to consume a day's worth of calories in a Tuesday afternoon. The gooey blondies studded with white chocolate chunks and crunchy Biscoff cookies (or biscuits, as Anna would say) are super easy to make, and if you want even more of the spiced, caramel-y cookie flavor, you can drizzle melted Biscoff cookie butter over the top. While the cookies may lose their crunch if you wait too long to eat the bars, the flavor intensifies over time, so these babies taste even better the next day. That is, if you don't eat them all on that Tuesday afternoon.

1. Preheat the oven to 325°F. Lightly grease and line a baking pan with foil or parchment paper.

2. Break roughly half of the Biscoff cookies into smaller pieces, reserving 8 whole cookies for the topping.

3. In the bowl of an electric mixer, mix softened butter and both sugars until pale and fluffy, about 3 minutes. Add vanilla and eggs, one at a time, scraping the bowl well after each addition. Mix until combined, about 1 to 2 minutes.

4. Add flour and salt, and using a spatula or wooden spoon, gently mix all ingredients together until just combined. Fold in chopped white chocolate and crushed Biscoff cookies. Transfer the batter to the lined baking pan and smooth the top using the back of a spoon or spatula.

5. Place the Biscoff cookie butter spread in the microwave for about 15 seconds, then add small blobs on top of the blondie batter. Use a toothpick or chopstick to gently swirl the spread into the rest of the batter.

6. Top the blondies with the remaining 8 cookies and bake for 25 to 30 minutes, until golden but still slightly wobbly in the middle. Do not overbake. When inserting a toothpick in the middle, it should come out with crumbs attached.

7. Let cool in pan for 20 minutes, then transfer to the refrigerator for at least an hour. Once cooled completely, slice into 9 pieces. Drizzle more melted cookie butter spread across the top, if desired.

CHAPTER 5

Things You Probably Shouldn't Eat with Your Hands

BROWN SUGAR PEACH COBBLER 126
Tieghan Gerard, food blogger and cookbook author (*Half Baked Harvest*)

RHUBARB CHEESECAKE 129
Erin Jeanne McDowell, from *The Fearless Baker*

CREAMY COCONUT CHEESECAKE WITH DULCE DE LECHE 130
Dev Amadeo, baking blogger (*The Yellow Butterfly*)

BUTTER PECAN CINNAMON BUNS 132
Ashley Manila, baking blogger (*Baker by Nature*)

GRAPEFRUIT TIRAMISU 134
Anne Ng and Jeremy Mandrell, Bakery Lorraine in Austin, TX

CLASSIC CRÈME BRÛLÉE 137
Jeff Osaka, chef/restaurateur in Denver, CO

CHOCOLATE CROISSANT BREAD PUDDING WITH FRESH CHANTILLY CREAM 139
Wiltshire Pantry Bakery & Café in Louisville, KY

CHOCOLATE SOUFFLÉS WITH CHOCOLATE SAUCE 140
Hedda Gioia Dowd and Cherif Brahmi, owners of rise n°1 restaurant in Dallas, TX

Brown Sugar Peach Cobbler

Tieghan Gerard, food blogger and cookbook author (*Half Baked Harvest*)

Makes one 12-inch cobbler

4 tablespoons (½ stick) salted butter

5 to 6 ripe but firm peaches, thinly sliced (about 6 cups sliced)

1 cup light brown sugar, divided

1 tablespoon bourbon (optional)

2 teaspoons vanilla extract

1 cup all-purpose flour

¼ cup finely ground pecans

2 teaspoons baking powder

1 teaspoon cinnamon

½ cup (1 stick) salted butter, melted

½ cup whole milk

cinnamon sugar for dusting

Special equipment:

12-inch oven-safe skillet

I don't think that many people outside of Colorado know that we grow the best peaches. They come from teeny-tiny Palisade (population: 2,700) on the western slope of the state, and they're just the juiciest, sweetest, most fragrant little treasures. So when searching for the best peach cobbler recipe, I looked to a fellow Coloradoan who's also intimately acquainted with these exceptional peaches: Tieghan Gerard, the chef/baker behind the crazy-popular Half Baked Harvest blog and cookbooks.

Tieghan's cobbler is easy to make but still filled with special touches like toasty brown butter, nutty pecans, and, if you so choose, a jolt of bourbon. The tastiness of everything involved is so cellular-level ingrained that it's pretty much impossible to screw up this dessert. And while Palisade peaches are certainly the best way to enjoy the cobbler, any peaches will do, even frozen.

1. Preheat the oven to 400°F. Add 4 tablespoons butter to skillet set over medium heat. Allow the butter to brown until it smells toasty and is a deep golden brown, stirring often, about 3 to 4 minutes.

2. Remove from heat and add peaches, ½ cup brown sugar, bourbon, and vanilla, tossing to combine. Transfer to oven and bake for 10 to 15 minutes. Reduce oven to 375°F.

3. Meanwhile, in a large bowl, whisk together flour, ground pecans, baking powder, cinnamon, and the remaining ½ cup brown sugar. Add 1 stick melted butter and milk, mixing until just combined.

4. Remove peaches from oven and dollop the batter over the peaches. Dust with cinnamon sugar and bake 25 to 30 minutes, or until golden on top. Let cool for 5 minutes and serve warm or at room temperature, probably with ice cream on top.

Rhubarb Cheesecake

Erin Jeanne McDowell, cookbook author and baker

Makes one 9-inch cheesecake

For the crust:

2 cups fine oatmeal cookie crumbs

3 tablespoons unsalted butter, melted

For the filling:

3 cups chopped rhubarb (plus extra stalks for garnish, if desired)

¼ cup granulated sugar

32 ounces cream cheese, room temperature

1½ cups granulated sugar with 2 teaspoons vanilla extract mixed in (vanilla sugar!)

5 large eggs

Besides being on the millennial pink spectrum, the appeal of this cheesecake is in the rhubarb. Instead of using an acid like lemon juice to give the cheesecake its firm-but-fluffy texture, Erin brilliantly swaps in rhubarb syrup. The rhubarb gently helps with the texture, the taste, and that oh-so-trendy blush pink color. Bonus: The rhubarb ribbons make for the prettiest-ever DIY topping that requires no talent whatsoever.

1. Preheat the oven to 350°F. To make the crust, mix the cookie crumbs and butter in a medium bowl. Press the mixture evenly into the bottom and slightly up the sides of a 9-inch springform pan.

2. Bake the crust until lightly golden, 10 to 12 minutes. Let the crust cool to room temperature, then transfer the springform pan (secured with oven bags, foil, or whatever your water bath-proofing method of choice) to a large roasting pan. Turn the oven temperature down to 325°F.

3. Heat a kettle of water to use for the water bath. While that heats up, combine rhubarb and ¼ cup sugar in a medium saucepan, tossing to mix. Cook over medium heat, stirring occasionally, until the rhubarb is very tender, 7 to 9 minutes. Let cool slightly, then puree with an immersion or regular blender until very smooth. You should end up with 1½ cups puree. Let cool to room temperature.

4. Transfer the cooled rhubarb puree to a food processor, add the cream cheese, vanilla sugar, and eggs, and process the mixture until very smooth, 1 to 2 minutes, pausing occasionally to scrape down the bowl.

5. Pour the custard into the cooled crust. Carefully pour enough hot water from the kettle into the roasting pan to come about halfway up the sides of the springform pan. Transfer the roasting pan to the oven and bake the cheesecake until the edges are set but the center still jiggles slightly when you shake the pan, 60 to 75 minutes.

6. Leave the cheesecake in the water bath to cool for 30 minutes, then transfer the springform pan to the refrigerator and chill thoroughly, at least 2 hours.

7. To make the garnish, fill a medium bowl with ice water. Use a sharp peeler to peel long strips from the stalks of rhubarb and transfer them to the ice water—this will help the strips curl up. After about 1 minute in the ice water, drain well on several layers of paper towels. Place on top of cheesecake just before serving.

Creamy Coconut Cheesecake with Dulce de Leche

Dev Amadeo, baking blogger (*The Yellow Butterfly*)

Makes one 9-inch cheesecake

For the crust:

10 tablespoons (1¼ sticks) unsalted butter

½ cup pistachios, optional

8 ounces (or 15 whole crackers) graham crackers, broken into small pieces

3 tablespoons sugar

For the cheesecake:

5 8-ounce packages cream cheese, room temperature

1¾ cups sugar

3 tablespoons all-purpose flour

1 tablespoon freshly squeezed lemon juice

¼ cup coconut milk, full fat

1½ to 2 teaspoons coconut extract

5 large eggs, room temperature,

2 large egg yolks, room temperature

For the Italian meringue:

½ lemon, to rub bowl and attachment

2 large egg whites, room temperature

½ teaspoon cream of tartar

½ cup water

1 cup sugar

Maybe it's because she lives in the coconut paradise that is Puerto Rico, or maybe it's because Dev Amadeo is just a flavor genius, but whisking a little coconut milk into cheesecake batter is Nobel Prize–worthy. Besides the coconutty kick, it adds creaminess, and with cheesecake you can never have too much creaminess.

If an uber-velvety, impeccably sweet/tangy cheesecake wasn't enough on its own, Dev then crowns her treasure with not just fresh fruit, not just dulce de leche, but also Italian meringue. Unfamiliar with Italian meringue? Unlike its Swiss and French cousins, the Italian iteration is a sturdy, stand-alone meringue. It's like a super satiny, less sweet, more aerated frosting, and once you make it, you'll want to put it on everything. But start with this cheesecake.

1. Spray bottom of a 9-inch springform pan or pie dish with nonstick spray. If using a springform pan, cover the bottom with a few pieces of aluminum foil until at least half the pan from the bottom up is covered. (You don't want water from the water bath getting in.) Preheat the oven to 350°F.

2. Place the 1¼ sticks of butter for the crust in a small saucepan and heat on medium-low until just melted. Remove from heat. Place pistachios in the bowl of a food processor and grind. Add the graham crackers, breaking them in pieces with your hands before throwing in. Add the sugar and run the processor until the crackers are crumbs. With the processor running, pour in the melted butter. Mix until crumbs are moist, about 10 to 15 seconds.

3. Transfer to baking pan. Press onto the bottom and up sides, until the crumbs are evenly distributed and you've reached your desired height. Bake for 6 minutes. Let cool.

4. Increase the oven to 425°F. In the bowl of a stand mixer with whisk attachment (or medium bowl with hand mixer), beat the 5 boxes of cream cheese for 2 to 3 minutes on low speed, until cream cheese is completely smooth. Add 1¾ cups sugar and mix for 1 minute. Decrease speed to lowest setting and add the flour, lemon juice, coconut milk, and coconut extract. Add the eggs and yolks one at a time, incorporating each fully before adding the next. Stop and scrape down the sides of your bowl and mix 30 seconds to 1 minute, until mixture is smooth and everything is well incorporated.

5. Pour mixture into baked crust. Place pan in a baking tray (a large casserole dish or even turkey roasting pan works well) and fill the tray with water until halfway up pan, making sure the water doesn't rise above the

For topping:

**¼ cup dulce de leche
or caramel sauce**

fresh fruit, optional

foil. Bake for 7 minutes, then decrease temperature to 275°F and bake for 1 hour and 10 minutes, until it looks set around the edges but still a little wobbly in center. Turn off oven and open oven door halfway. After about 2 minutes, remove from oven.

6. Let cheesecake cool, then place in fridge. It should chill for 6 to 8 hours, or, even better, overnight.

7. To make the Italian meringue, first make sure your bowl and whisk attachment are clean and free from grease. (Grease will prevent the egg whites from rising.) Rub the bottom and walls of the bowl and whisk attachment with half a lemon. Pour egg whites and cream of tartar into

the bowl, whisking on low speed for 30 seconds and then increasing the speed to medium until soft peaks form.

8. Meanwhile, combine water and sugar in a small saucepan. Heat over high heat and cook until a candy thermometer reaches 240°F, about 3 to 4 minutes. With the mixer running, pour the sugar syrup into the meringue. Whisk until meringue reaches room temperature, 3 to 5 minutes. When the bowl feels cool on the outside, it's ready.

9. Remove cheesecake from springform pan (if using) and top with meringue, dulce de leche or caramel, and fresh fruit, if desired.

Butter Pecan Cinnamon Buns

Ashley Manila, baking blogger (*Baker by Nature*)

Makes 12 rolls

For the dough:

1 cup whole milk

4 tablespoons (½ stick) unsalted butter, very soft

3½ cups all-purpose flour, divided

1 .25-ounce package rapid rise yeast

3 tablespoons granulated sugar

¾ teaspoon salt

1 large egg, room temperature

For the filling:

1 cup light brown sugar

1 tablespoon ground cinnamon

¾ teaspoon ground ginger

¼ teaspoon nutmeg

¼ teaspoon ground cloves

½ cup (1 stick) butter, very soft

For the butter pecans:

½ cup (1 stick) unsalted butter

¾ cup dark brown sugar, packed

¼ teaspoon ground cinnamon

⅓ cup heavy cream

¼ teaspoon salt

1½ cups pecan halves

½ cup pecans, roughly chopped

2 teaspoons vanilla extract

I used to think that cinnamon buns were made by magic. They just seemed so impossibly fluffy, so stickily delicious, that they had to be made by centaurs or sprites or some other enchanted creature. Spoiler alert: You do not need to be a mythical being to make cinnamon buns. The ingredients are all pretty simple, and the technique difficulty maxes out at flattening dough and then rolling it up into the cinnamony, sugary pinwheels that melt in our mouths. The crunchy topping of spiced butter pecans in this recipe only adds to the magic.

1. Lightly grease a 9x13-inch baking dish with nonstick baking spray. Set aside. In a small saucepan, carefully heat the milk over medium-high until it just comes to a boil. Remove from heat and add in the butter. Stir until it is completely melted, then let mixture cool until it's 115 to 120°F.

2. In the bowl of a stand mixer fitted with the dough hook attachment, combine 2½ cups of the flour with the yeast, sugar, and salt, using a whisk. Whisk in the egg. Slowly pour in the milk/butter mixture, whisking well to combine.

3. Using the dough hook, turn the mixer on low speed. Add the remaining flour, ¼ cup at a time, mixing well after each addition and using a spatula to scrape down the sides as needed. Once all of the flour has been added, increase the mixer to medium speed and beat for 5 minutes.

4. Remove the dough from the bowl. On a lightly floured surface, gently knead the dough into a smooth and neat ball, about 5 or 6 times. Place the ball of dough back into the bowl and cover the bowl tightly with a piece of

Saran wrap. Set aside for 60 minutes, or until the dough has doubled in size.

5. For the filling: In a medium-sized bowl, mix together brown sugar, spices, and softened butter until evenly combined. It should resemble a thick paste.

6. Once the dough has risen, it's time to assemble! Roll out the dough into a very large rectangle, about 16x9 inches. Spread the filling onto the middle of the dough, leaving a barrier around the tops and sides. Tightly roll up the dough (jellyroll style), and gently pinch the seams to seal. Using unscented dental floss or a serrated knife, cut the roll into 12 equal-size pieces.

7. Place the pieces, cut side up, in the prepared pan. Cover again tightly with Saran wrap and let rise for another 30 minutes. While they're rising, preheat the oven to 350°F.

8. Once risen, bake for 18 to 20 minutes, or until lightly browned on the tops and edges.

9. While the rolls are baking, make the butter pecans. In a small saucepan over medium heat, melt the butter. Add in the brown sugar and cook, stirring

with a whisk, until the sugar has melted and the mixture is bubbling, about 2 minutes. Add in the cinnamon, heavy cream, and salt, and whisk to combine. Add in the pecans and, using a rubber spatula, fold them into the liquid mixture until they're completely coated. Remove from heat and stir in the vanilla.

10. Allow buns to cool a few minutes, then top with butter pecans and serve!

Grapefruit Tiramisu

Anne Ng and Jeremy Mandrell, Bakery Lorraine in Austin, TX

Makes about 6 individual portions, or one large baking dish

For the ladyfingers:

granulated sugar, divided into ⅓ cup (sugar A) and 3¼ tablespoons (sugar B)

3 egg yolks

4 egg whites

⅓ teaspoon cream of tartar

⅓ teaspoon egg white powder

⅔ cup all-purpose flour

more granulated sugar, for sprinkling

For the mascarpone anglaise:

pinch of plain gelatin

enough cold water to dissolve the gelatin, maybe 1/10 cup

⅔ cup heavy cream

1 vanilla bean or 1 tablespoon vanilla extract

just under ¼ cup granulated sugar

2 egg yolks

7 ounces mascarpone cheese

½ cup heavy cream

For the grapefruit syrup:

1 cup grapefruit juice (you can use juice from fresh grapefruit that you'll supreme)

½ cup granulated sugar

zest from 1 grapefruit

grapefruit suprèmes for garnish (remove the bitter white membrane as best you can so you're left with only the sweet, pink little wedges)

Forget everything you think you know about tiramisu. OK, maybe not everything—the ladyfingers can stay. And the mascarpone cream. But ditch the espresso and replace it with grapefruit. Yes, grapefruit. Preferably of the Texas variety, which Anne Ng describes as ethereal, a whole other fruit unto itself. The acid and cream are a great match, and once you take a bite, you'll see why this is a customer favorite at Bakery Lorraine. It's a zippier take on the classic dessert, and who doesn't like a little more zip?

1. To make the ladyfingers, preheat the oven to 375°F, high fan. Line a baking sheet with parchment paper. Whip sugar A and egg yolks in a large bowl until fluffy and almost white in color.

2. In a separate bowl, whip sugar B, egg whites, cream of tartar, and egg white powder until you get a meringue with stiff peaks. Sift flour and gently fold into the whipped yolk mixture. Add the meringue.

3. Transfer mixture to a piping bag with a large plain tip (or a good old-fashioned baggie with an edge cut off also works) and pipe onto a baking sheet in sections about 5 inches long and 1.5 inches wide. Sprinkle with granulated sugar and bake for about 6 minutes, until the outside is light brown.

4. For the mascarpone anglaise, bloom gelatin by sprinkling the gelatin powder in cold water; stir. Let it sit for a few minutes to allow gelatin to hydrate.

5. In a saucepan, combine cream and vanilla extract (or bean and empty pod). Bring to a boil and then lower heat. Meanwhile, in a mixing bowl,

whisk sugar and egg yolks. Pour half of the hot cream, just a little bit at a time, into the sugar-yolk mixture, whisking continuously. Then pour the egg-yolk mixture into the rest of the hot cream and put saucepan back over low heat.

6. Using a wooden spoon, slowly and continuously stir the mixture until you reach 185°F, or about 10 minutes. The mixture should be thick enough to coat the back of the wooden spoon. Turn off the heat, add the bloomed gelatin mix, and stir until it completely dissolves. Strain into a large metal bowl and cool down in an ice bath.

7. While that's cooling, make the grapefruit syrup by combining and heating the juice, sugar, and zest in a saucepan until all the sugar has dissolved. Cool down to room temperature.

8. Once the anglaise is cool, combine it a little bit at a time with your mascarpone cheese, using a whisk. Don't be aggressive with the whisk, to avoid curdling the cheese. Make sure there are no lumps, and gently whisk until everything is just combined.

9. Whip the ½ cup heavy cream until it forms soft peaks, and fold into the anglaise.

10. To assemble: spread a light layer of mascarpone cream on the bottom of your dish, just enough to cover it. Next, dip the ladyfingers in the grapefruit syrup for a few seconds, then immediately place over the cream layer. (If making individual portions, cut the ladyfingers into smaller pieces before dipping.) Keep repeating until the cream is covered in a single layer of ladyfingers. Then spread half of the remaining cream over the ladyfingers. Repeat the layering process with the rest of the ladyfingers. Spread the remaining cream on top and refrigerate for at least an hour to set. Before serving, garnish with grapefruit suprèmes.

Classic Crème Brûlée

Jeff Osaka, chef/restaurateur in Denver, CO

Makes six 8-ounce ramekins

1 quart heavy cream

1 vanilla bean (split, seeds scraped)

7 large egg yolks

1 cup sugar, divided (¾ cup for custard, ¼ cup for caramelized topping)

Special equipment:

kitchen torch

Before cupcakes, before Cronuts,® heck, before electric stand mixers ever even existed, there was crème brûlée. The four-ingredient dessert is so classic that it's hard to imagine a world without it, and luckily we won't ever have to unless we screw up the earth so badly that she decides to stop producing sugar cane and cows and, well, let's just not think about that right now. Anyway, crème brûlée is so lusciously elegant that you'd think it would be a pain to make, but so long as you're careful and don't scorch yourself, it can be done in five reasonably easy steps. Grab a strainer, some ramekins, and a kitchen torch and give it a go.

1. Preheat the oven to 325°F. Place the cream, vanilla bean, and its seeds into a medium saucepan set over medium-high heat and bring to a boil. Remove from heat, cover, and allow vanilla to steep for 15 to 20 minutes.

2. In a medium bowl, whisk together the egg yolks and ¾ cup sugar until well blended and just starting to turn pale yellow in color. Add the hot cream a little at a time, stirring continually to avoid scrambling the eggs.

3. Pour through a fine mesh strainer to capture any lumps of sugar, vanilla bean, or overcooked eggs.

4. Ladle the liquid equally into the six ramekins. Place ramekins in a large baking pan, and pour enough hot water into the pan to come ⅓ of the way up the sides of the ramekins. Cover with aluminum foil and bake just until the custard is set around the edges but still a little loose in the middle, approximately 40 to 45 minutes. Remove the ramekins from the pan and refrigerate at least 2 hours and up to 3 days.

5. For the caramelized topping, divide the remaining ¼ cup sugar equally among the ramekins and spread evenly on top. Using a torch, melt the sugar and form the crispy caramel top. (Be careful, as the sugar may splatter.) Allow the crème brûlée to sit for at least 5 minutes before serving.

Chocolate Croissant Bread Pudding with Fresh Chantilly Cream

Wiltshire Pantry Bakery & Café in Louisville, KY

Makes one 9x13-inch pan

For the bread pudding:

½ cup (1 stick) unsalted butter

1 cup sugar

2 teaspoons vanilla extract

½ teaspoon kosher salt

5 eggs

2½ cups heavy cream

4 chocolate or butter croissants—bonus points if they're from Wiltshire!

¾ cup chocolate chips

For the Chantilly cream:

2 cups heavy whipping cream

½ cup powdered sugar

½ teaspoon vanilla extract

While I think the Chantilly cream is the star of the show in this dish, let's not overlook the awesome fat-on-fat action that is chocolate croissants covered in more chocolate and drenched in sweetened, buttery, heavy cream. That definitely deserves some acknowledgement, and so there it is, acknowledged. But back to that Chantilly cream. Really, it's just a fancy way of saying sweetened, vanilla-spiked whipped cream, and it's easier to make than you think. You pour three ingredients in a bowl and hit go. That's it. That's all the effort needed to yield yourself a bowl full of scoopable, fluffy heaven.

1. Preheat the oven to 350°F. In a food processor, combine butter and sugar and process until well blended. Add vanilla and salt and pulse to combine. While the processor is running, crack eggs into the mixture. Turn off the processor and scrape down the sides. Add heavy cream and pulse to combine.

2. Lightly butter a 9x13-inch baking dish. Cut up the croissants into 1-inch pieces and layer in the pan. Scatter the chocolate chips over the top and gently mix to incorporate. Pour the egg mixture over the croissants and soak for 8 to 10 minutes. You will need to push the croissant pieces down to ensure even coverage of egg mixture.

3. Cover with foil and bake for 45 to 50 minutes. Remove foil and bake an additional 15 to 30 minutes, until top is golden and custard is set but still soft. Allow to cool and then dust with powdered sugar.

4. For the Chantilly cream, place all ingredients in the bowl of an electric mixer and mix on medium speed with the whip attachment until thick peaks form. Use immediately or store for up to 3 days and re-whip as needed.

Chocolate Soufflés with Chocolate Sauce

Hedda Gioia Dowd and Cherif Brahmi, owners of rise n°1 restaurant in Dallas, TX

Makes four 12-ounce ramekins

For the soufflés:

3 egg yolks

1¼ cups granulated sugar, divided

¼ cup flour

1 tablespoon cornstarch

2 cups whole milk, scalded

1 tablespoon unsweetened cocoa powder

10 large egg whites

butter for coating ramekins

sugar for coating ramekins

For the chocolate sauce:

1 cup heavy cream

1 cup half-and-half

½ cup granulated sugar

½ pound bittersweet chocolate morsels

powdered sugar, for garnish

Soufflés are eggy little miracles that remind us that all things are possible. Unfortunately, they've garnered an unfair reputation for being difficult to make, but trust me when I say that these magical chocolate clouds are worth trying at home, and you're more likely to get that rise if you follow this recipe from rise. (Oh snap, you cheekily-named soufflé restaurant, you!)

To maximize your chances at success, follow these cardinal laws of soufflé: 1. *Gently* fold the egg whites into the pastry cream using a rubber spatula. 2. Fill the ramekins to just over ¾ full so they have room to grow. Voilà! Chocolatey, eggy magic is yours for the tasting.

---

1. Preheat the oven to 375°F. Butter ramekins and, using a rolling motion, coat ramekins with sugar. Set aside.

2. For the soufflés, combine egg yolks, ¾ cup sugar, flour, and cornstarch in a small mixing bowl and whisk until smooth. Slowly add hot scalded milk to mixture, whisking constantly until milk is incorporated.

3. Transfer mixture into a non-aluminum saucepan and heat over medium heat. Stir constantly. Heat and stir until pastry cream thickens and boils, careful not to scorch the bottom. When it reaches a boil, pour into a storage container or bowl to cool. Stir occasionally to prevent skin from forming on top. Add cocoa and mix well. Set aside.

4. In the bowl of an electric mixer at high speed, beat egg whites. While beating, add remaining sugar. Beat until soft peaks form. With a rubber spatula, very gently fold egg whites and pastry cream into a bowl. Stir gently, then pour mixture into ramekins, keeping edges clean.

5. Place soufflés on lowest oven rack, leaving 6 to 8 inches above the ramekins to allow souffles to rise. Bake for 25 to 30 minutes, until tops are browned and it doesn't jiggle too much when gently shaken.

6. While the soufflés are baking, make the chocolate sauce. Place cream, half-and-half, granulated sugar, and chocolate in a medium saucepan and heat over medium heat, mixing well. Bring sauce to a boil while whipping occasionally. Remove from heat when it reaches a boil.

7. Dust tops of soufflés with powdered sugar and pour chocolate sauce over them before serving.

RECOMMENDED READING

Want to read more from these amazing bakers? Of course you do! Here are the cookbooks and blogs you need for more incredible recipes and inspiration.

Books

Dominique Ansel, *Everyone Can Bake* and *Dominique Ansel: The Secret Recipes,* Simon & Schuster

Tessa Arias, *The Ultimate Cookie Handbook*

Daniel Boulud, *Daniel Boulud's Café Boulud Cookbook,* Scribner; *My Best,* Ducasse Books; *Daniel's Dish,* Filipacchi Publishing; and *Daniel: My French Cuisine,* Grand Central Publishing

Joanne Chang, *Flour* and *Flour, Too,* Chronicle Books; *Myers + Chang At Home* and *Pastry Love,* Mariner Books

Courtney Cowan, *Milk Jar Cookies Bakebook,* Welcome Books

Jocelyn Delk Adams, *Grandbaby Cakes,* Agate Surrey

Tieghan Gerard, *Half Baked Harvest* and *Super Simple,* Clarkson Potter

Hedda Gioia Dowd and Cherif Brahmi, *Rise to the Occasion,* Arcadia

Duff Goldman, *Super Good Baking for Kids,* HarperCollins; *Duff Bakes* and *Ace of Cakes,* William Morrow Cookbooks

Tanya Holland, *Brown Sugar Kitchen,* Chronicle Books and *New Soul Cooking,* Abrams

Sophie Kallinis LaMontagne and Katherine Kallinis Berman, *The Cupcake Diaries* and *Sweet Celebrations,* HarperOne

Agatha Kulaga and Erin Patinkin, *Ovenly,* Park Row

Erin Jeanne McDowell, *The Fearless Baker* and *The Book on Pie,* Mariner Books

Rebecca Rather, *The Pastry Queen, Pastry Queen Parties,* and *The Pastry Queen Christmas,* Ten Speed Press

Courtney Rich, *CAKE by Courtney,* Courtney Rich/Rich Creative Group

Allison Robicelli, *Robicelli's: a Love Story, with Cupcakes,* Viking Books Studio; *Back to the Future: The Official Hill Valley Cookbook* and *WWE: The Official Cookbook,* Insight Editions

Mindy Segal, *Cookie Love,* Ten Speed Press

Christina Tosi, *All About Cake, Momofuku Milk Bar, Milk Bar: Kids Only, Milk Bar Life,* and *MasterChef Junior Bakes!,* Clarkson Potter; *Every Cake Has a Story,* Dial Books

Tracy Wilk, *#BakeItForward,* BookBaby

Blogs

Majed Ali, thecinnaman.com

Dev Amadeo, devamadeo.com

Tessa Arias, handletheheat.com

Jocelyn Delk Adams, grandbaby-cakes.com

Astrid Field, thesweetrebellion.co.za

Tieghan Gerard, halfbakedharvest.com

Duff Goldman, duff.com

Cambrea Gordon, cambreabakes.com

Kimberlee Ho, kickassbaker.com

Ashley Manila, bakerbynature.com

Liz Marek, sugargeekshow.com

Erin Jeanne McDowell, erinjeannemcdowell.com

Courtney Rich, cakebycourtney.com

Christina Tosi, christinatosi.com

Tracy Wilk, cheftracywilk.com

Chelsey White, chelsweets.com

Anna Wierzbinska, annabanana.co

Kate Wood, thewoodandspoon.com

ACKNOWLEDGMENTS

A huge thank you to the incredible bakers and pastry chefs who shared their recipes with me. There would be no cookbook without them, and I am so grateful to all of the kind souls who helped me turn my 50 Things idea into an actual, real-life book. I thank you for your kitchen talents and sweet generosity.

Greg McBoat went well beyond photographing so many of these treats—he turned my baking disasters into the beautiful photos you see here, all while keeping me sane and talking me down after I screwed up yet another cake/pie/cheesecake/insert-pretty-much-any-dessert here. His talents, patience, encouragement, and kindness are so appreciated, and I couldn't have done this book with anyone else.

And to my two little taste-testers (and the one bigger taste-tester): there's no one I'd rather bake for.

ABOUT THE AUTHOR

Allyson Reedy is a dessert-obsessed food writer and restaurant critic in Denver, Colorado. When she's not taste-testing or checking out new restaurants for a story, she's probably tripping over her pug in her home kitchen while trying out cookie recipes. Oh, and eating batter and dough by the fistful before her kids ask to lick the bowl; there's a lot of that happening, too.